The Complete Book to
Develop Your I.Q.

Gilles Azzopardi

D1254832

foulsham
LONDON • NEW YORK • TORONTO • SYDNEY

foulsham

Bennetts Close, Cippenham, Berks SL1 5AP

Other titles of interest:
Measure Your I.Q.
Succeed at I.Q. Tests

ANSWER: THE SEQUENCE IS PRIME NUMBERS.
EACH NUMBER IS OBTAINED BY TAKING THE
PRIME NUMBER, CUBING IT, THEN SUBTRACTING
ITS OWN VALUE.

$$2^3 - 2 = 6 \qquad 7^3 - 7 = 336$$
$$3^3 - 3 = 24 \qquad 11^3 - 11 = 1320$$
$$5^3 - 5 = 120 \qquad 13^3 - 13 = 2184$$

ANSWER: THERE ARE 15 IN THE DRAWING,
AND 10 HAVE A DIFFERENT SHAPE.

ISBN 0-572-01934-3

This English language version copyright © 1993
W. Foulsham & Co. Ltd.
Originally published by
Marabout, Alleur, Belgium © Marabout.

Phototypeset in Great Britain by Typesetting Solutions, Slough, Berks.
Printed in Great Britain by St Edmundsbury Press Ltd,
Bury St Edmunds, Suffolk.

CONTENTS

INTELLECTUAL DEVELOPMENT

Intelligence is important. It is a quality, a virtue and an ability, rather than just another function. It is a gift from Nature (or a Divine Grace) like beauty and strength, and something to be envied. All of us have at some time doubted our intelligence and would like to be more confident of our talents.

Can one become more intelligent?

This question, which has no doubt been asked thousands of times around the world, invariably gets the same mixture of replies. Firstly, there are those who believe that intelligence stems from God (or Nature), belonging to that inborn domain within us all that depends essentially on heredity and is fundamentally unchangeable. However, most of us believe that man is capable of improvement, and becomes more capable by his very efforts to improve himself.

Finally there are those people who believe that intelligence is acquired through life's experiences, and is fundamentally dependent on one's social background. Despite all these different theories, the majority of people are convinced that at birth, man is as equal in intelligence as he is in human rights.

Is intelligence hereditary?

The differences we find between the intellectual performances of individual people suggest that intelligence is above all hereditary. Indeed, these differences cannot be explained by the individual's cultural and social backgrounds alone. The problem is that the thesis that intelligence is essentially hereditary has implications, often of a racist nature.

W. Stockley, Nobel Prize Winner in Physics and inventor of the transistor, even proposed sterlising his black American compatriots at the end of the 50's because they were obtaining poor results in I.Q. tests. When we know that the results of these tests are directly related to social-economic conditions (degree of socio-professional integration, schooling, economical position, etc.) which he could not ignore, one doubts his ideological stand.

Nowadays American researchers once again claim to have scientifically shown the dominating role heredity plays in intelligence. The results of their work, published at the end of 1988 in the British scientific journal *Nature* seemed to prove it. Simplified, their results showed that adopted children's performances in I.Q. tests were closer to their natural mothers' performances than the intellectual level of their adoptive family.

But when one knows that the adoptive system in the States makes sure that there is no great gap between the family of origin and the adoptive family, the significance of these works is reduced. The role heredity plays in intelligence has still not been precisely assessed. Nevertheless, most specialists are reasonably agreed that in certain aspects, intellectual ability is hereditary.

How influential is your background?

You don't have to be a genius to notice that children from better social classes generally obtain better scholastic results than those from underprivileged backgrounds. These observations have been made from studies made on the intellectual levels of school children. In general, the child's performance in I.Q. tests is directly related to their father's socio-professional standing.

The table below shows the average I.Q. level of 100,000 pupils from 6-14 years old, in relation to their father's profession. These studies were carried out by the French National Institute of Demographic Studies, and published in 1973.

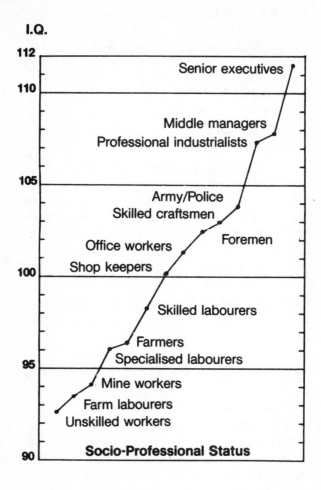

More recently, the results from a study by the French National Centre for Scientific Research* confirm the overwhelming influence social background has on intellectual development. The I.Q. of children adopted before the age of six months by privileged families is, on average, 12 points greater than that of children adopted by working class families.

The role social background plays has been proved for a long time. However, it is difficult to precisely measure its effects because all these evaluations are directly tied to the nature of intelligence itself.

What is intelligence?

In the past, intelligence has been defined in countless ways, from a 'natural ability' to a 'divine power' and a 'vital function'. Nowadays this sort of simple definition has more or less been dismissed. Intelligence is being defined from a different approach that is concerned more with judgemental value than mere description.

Most specialists in the different areas concerned (anthropology, neuro-biology, psychology, etc.) more or less agree on two distinctions:

— The first corresponds to the distinction between genetic inheritance (genotype) and individual characters (phenotype).

— The second differentiates two large forms of intelligence: abstract/concrete, theoretical/practical, logical/empirical, formal/technical, rational/sensorial.

---

*These results were published in August 1989 in the British journal, *Nature*.

Intelligence and genetic inheritance

The distinction between the two categories of intelligence, one concerned with inheritance, the other with background influence during an individual's development, has numerous advantages.

For example, it avoids the conflict between heredity and social background. Consequently, the question as to whether all men are intellectually equal, or whether there are groups of people with a superior intelligence, becomes very secondary. One no longer wonders whether eskimos are superior to the peoples of Papua New Guinea or to the Westerners. The real problem lies in working out whether the intellectual potential of one or the other is more adapted to resolve inherent difficulties in their particular culture, and how they set about to overcome them.

Intelligence and individual characters

From this point of view, individual intelligence appears to be something personally acquired. It is without doubt determined by the different background influences during a person's development. The same genetic inheritance, when exposed to different external influences can, therefore, create individual characters with different intelligences.

But the acquisition is also affected by the realisation of this experience. To ask whether intelligence can be perfected by itself, or whether one can only learn to use it better, seems like another false question. Nowadays, no one denies that intelligence can be improved and indeed, that it should be. Developing the intelligence is as indispensable to individuals as for organisations being endlessly confronted by a more complex world.

The real question is how to do this; what is the best method to develop one's intelligence? The method depends first and foremost on the type of intelligence concerned, sensory-motor or rational, concrete or abstract.

Concrete intelligence

Concrete intelligence is tied in much more with instinct and innate ideas, than to what is acquired. What differentiates men from animals is that the former are able to make tools, whereas animals simply make use of things already made.

The essential period for the development of concrete intelligence is during childhood. It is during this time that the individual learns to solve all the practical problems posed by his environment. Intellectual development is therefore directly related to social, cultural and family background. The richer the environment, variety of situations, stimulations and experiences, the better the development. Monotonous family life, lack of social contacts and cultural stimulation lead to poor development.

During adolescence and adulthood, concrete intelligence scarcely develops at all, and the brain is concerned with learning new techniques and adapting to new situations, both environmental and material.

Abstract intelligence

In modern society, abstract intelligence has taken over from concrete intelligence. Modern day man is rather to primitive man, what adults are to children. He has discovered all the basic techniques, and great inventions now belong to the domain of ideas and theory.

Nowadays the term 'intelligence' refers more to understanding and reason, or even communication or creation, than to practical or good sense. An examination of concrete intelligence quickly suggests that several abilities are employed; those of changing the approach to solve a problem, using instruments or devices for fabricating tools.

On the other hand, any study of abstract intelligence leads more directly to the question of the nature of intelligence. What is it? Is it a single faculty open to different uses, or a combination of different faculties which contribute to reaching a single objective?

At present, there are the same number of supporters for one theory as for the other. One group is trying to prove a single all embracing intelligence, the other a composite intelligence.

Universal intelligence

The notion of one all embracing intelligence is obvious. Everyone feels its existence at some time. It arises from the fact that we are all conscious beings capable of abstraction. Various studies of intelligence have confirmed this feeling. One can observe and measure one common factor amongst all the different types of tests used to evaluate intelligence. Intelligence doesn't allow itself to be reduced to a series of particular abilities; intelligence is a constant characteristic.

Composite intelligence

At the end of the 19th Century, intelligence was not only defined as a single faculty, but also as a combination of distinct faculties. From this moment onwards, intelligence started to be fragmented and described in a series of aptitudes: perception, memory, language, etc., being the more basic; understanding, reasoning, criticism and invention being the more sophisticated.

According to the specialists, the number of components that make up intelligence varies from 0 to 120, and sometimes more.

The components of intelligence

Certain components, seven in all, are recognised by the majority of intelligence "professionals".
• a spatial component (perception and the ability to distinguish between two- and three-dimensional spatial shapes).
• a perception component (identification of any given shape inside a complex one).
• a memory component (memorising and recollecting objects without any logical connection).
• a numerical component (manipulation of numbers).
• a verbal component (comprehension of language).
• a lexical component (manipulation of vocabulary).
• a reasoning component (induction and deduction).

Intellectual functioning

Single or composite intelligence can, in both hypotheses, be conceived and described in terms of intellectual functioning. Since the 50's intellectual functioning has often been compared to the functioning of a computer, though greatly superior.
   The brain and the machine do, it must be said, have certain things in common:
• Differentiating between simple and elaborate symbols (images, concepts and models).
• Making the links according to the rules of logic, arithmetic for calculations, semantics for language.
• Carrying out complex tasks while performing the sequences of elementary procedures with great rapidity.
• Accomplishing various tasks, mobilising and adpating resources and methods to achieve different objectives.
   This is where the similarity ends. Thanks to its constitution and abilities the human brain outclasses the most advanced computers.

The functioning of the brain

The cerebral machine does, in fact, have nothing in common with the computer. Made up of about 100 thousand million neurones (nerve cells), linked together by approximately 100,000 billion synapses (neurone contacts), the cerebral machine allows an almost unlimited number of combinations, something the computer cannot begin to equal.

The electro-chemical energy (electrical in the neurones, chemical in the synapses) that runs through the brain can take on an almost infinite number of circuits.

Is intelligence programmed?

For a long time the brain/computer analogy led to the belief that intelligence was programmed. Neuronal circuits would be predetermined, organised once and for all in a certain way, and the brain would respond like a programmed computer. Consequently, the information would be established by the outside world.

In 1978, Gerald M. Edelman, an American (Nobel Prize for Medicine in 1972) put forward proof to support a theory that revolutionised the research world. A theory that, in brief, states that 'information is not established from the outside world, but is created in the brain itself'. For, in reality, the neuronal and nervous connections are never the same in one brain and another: there are no (and never will be) two identical brains.

Each brain is unique, and creates its own capacity to think, at any given moment, from its environment.

Can you develop your intelliegence?

With each brain being unique, each has its own methods of functioning and learning. Intelligence in itself is not something fixed. It is permanently re-creating itself from experiences past and present. It is capable of reinventing solutions to problems posed, at any instant.

Intelligence is dynamic, and open to development and training.

How to become super-intelligent

This method is made up of an assessment programme, a short and a long programme, and finishes with advice on your lifestyle.

The exercises we propose, 360 in all, and their effect as a whole have been created to allow you to increase your intellectual level and your performance in the specific areas that make up intelligence.

These areas are:
• PERCEPTION (spatial and perception).
• LANGUAGE (verbal and lexical).
• LOGIC (reasoning).
• NUMBERS (numerical).

In most of these activities, memory plays a certain role. But developing the memory is a whole new programme in itself.

ASSESS YOURSELF

The following test has been devised to allow you rapidly to evaluate your intellectual level and to understand your performance in different intellectual areas. There are four tests, each one containing 20 problems that you must solve, while at the same time strictly obeying the instructions. These tests are preceded by a series of examples to familiarise you with the sort of problems posed.

Instructions

These tests are only worthwhile if you strictly obey the following instructions:

• The time allowed for each test is 15 minutes. When this time is up, you may no longer complete or correct your answers.

• On the other hand, you can spend as much time as you like to study the examples given and if you want to, you can rest between each test.

• You must solve the problems mentally, without using any aids (dictionary, calculator, etc.). The pen and paper you use are only there to write down your answers.

• You must wait until you have finished all four tests before checking your answers.

Some Advice

You need just over an hour to take this test. Make sure you are in a good intellectual state. Wait until you are on form and choose a quiet area. Make yourself comfortable and disconnect the phone or put on the answering machine so as not to be disturbed.

You have 15 minutes per test to solve 20 problems; which is less than a minute per problem on average. Therefore you have no time to lose. Don't get stuck on a particular problem. Move on to the next one if you cannot find the solution within a reasonable time. But do not give up on a problem too quickly in the hope that the next one will be easier.

The best method is to solve as many problems as possible as quickly as you can so that you can go back to the ones you found difficult. It is almost impossible to solve all the problems in the time given. Do not worry, therefore, if at the end of a test you have not found all the solutions.

One last bit of advice. Put an alarm clock or stop-watch next to you before each test so as not to worry about time. Do not take the opportunity to re-read your answers between each test. You will start doubting, and all to no avail.

Examples : problems

These examples are designed to familiarise you with the types of problems that follow. Take time to study them, understand what they are asking, the logic in the solutions, your reply mechanism, and the reasons for your mistakes.

1. **Study the chessboard carefully for 30 seconds. Try and remember the position of each playing piece. Then cover the board.**

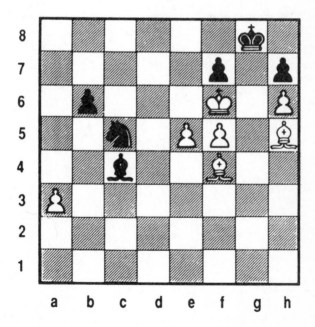

... and try to remember the position of the black knight.

2. Which figure, of the six shown below, completes the sequence?

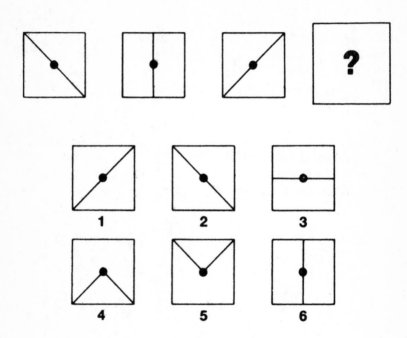

3. **Study the pyramids for 15 seconds. Then group together the ones that are the same size.**

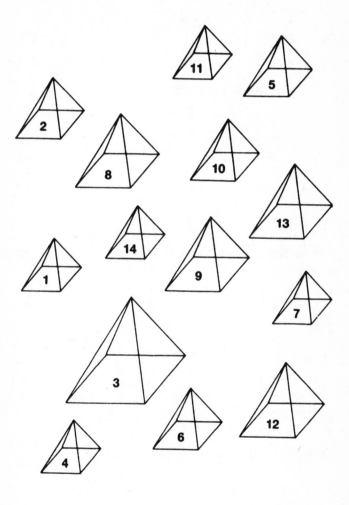

4. **Find a word which, when placed in the brackets, forms a different word with each preceding letter(s).**

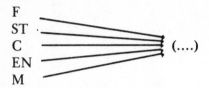

F
ST
C   (....)
EN
M

5. **Find the missing number.**

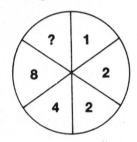

6. **Fill in the second line, using the first line as an example.**

    IMPOSE (SOON) WINNOW
    REPENT (....) MORTAL

7. **Find the missing number.**

    4   3   2   5
    9   5   3   11
    11   7   5   .

8. **Complete the sequence.**

    A C A E A G A K A M A .

9. **Find the two missing numbers.**

    3   6   12   15   30   33   . .   . .

10. **Study the top figure closely for 30 seconds. Then cover it up and find the one that is identical to it, from the four shown below.**

1

2

3

4

11. Study the two shapes shown below. The same shape is shown twice, once in 3-dimensions, and then flat. Shade in the areas that should be black on the second figure, to show its volume.

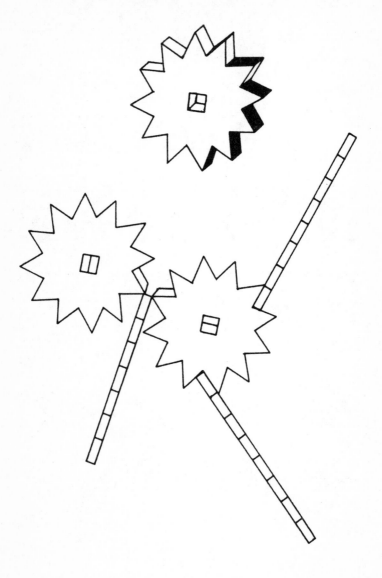

12. Fill in the missing domino.

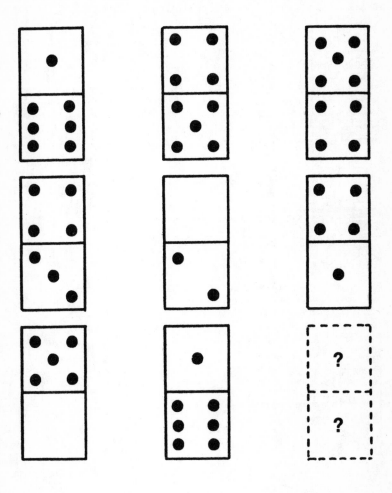

13. Spot the difference between these two figures.

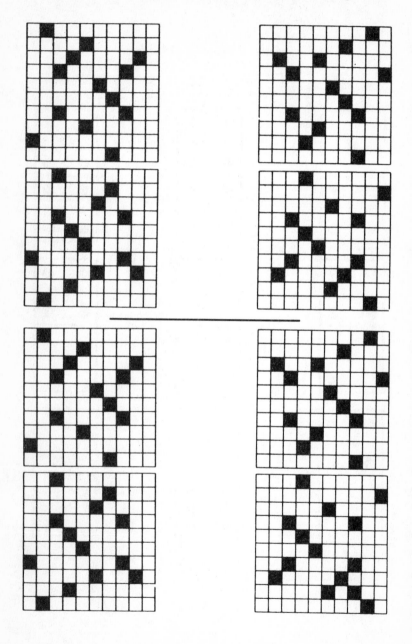

14. Study this mosaic. When turned 90° anti-clockwise, which figure ('a', 'b', 'c' or 'd') does it become?

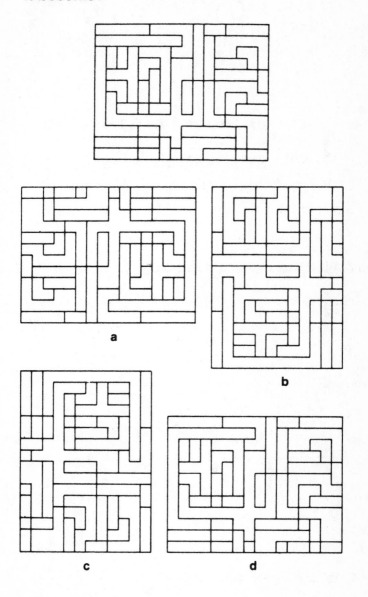

15. $\dfrac{360}{18} = 20$ ☐ YES ☐ NO

$4317 \times 3 = 12951$ ☐ YES ☐ NO

$728 + 452 = 1180$ ☐ YES ☐ NO

$913 - 357 = 555$ ☐ YES ☐ NO

16. Which word completes the following sentence?

'A word is to a sentence what a letter is to . . .'.

the mind, a word, writing, a name, the alphabet, a number.

17. Find the missing number.

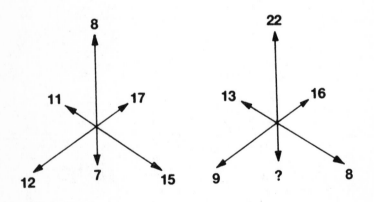

18. Which is the odd one out?

hemp, cotton, jute, flax, raffia, silk.

19. Which figure is the odd one out?

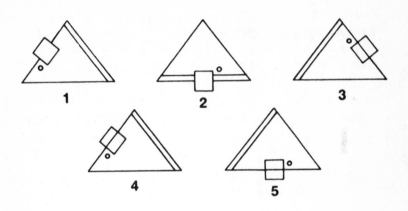

20. Which figure, of the five shown below, completes the sequence?

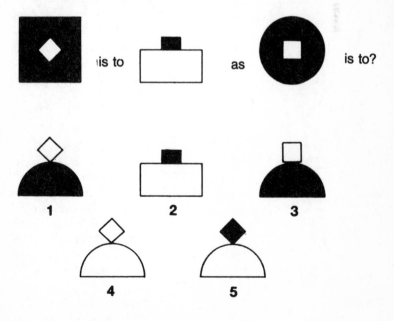

Examples: solutions

PROBLEM No.	SOLUTION	EXPLANATION
1	C5	You must remember the letter and number of the coordinates of each piece.
2	3	The line moves 45° clockwise each time.

PROBLEM No.	SOLUTION	EXPLANATION
3	(3) (8, 9, 12, 13) (2, 5, 6, 10) (1, 4, 7, 11, 14)	There are four different sizes of pyramid.
4	able	Which forms the words: fable, stable, cable, enable and lable.
5	32	Each number is obtained by multiplying together the two numbers preceding it. $1 \times 2 = 2$, $2 \times 2 = 4$, $2 \times 4 = 8$, $4 \times 8 = 32$.
6	neat	The first letter of the word in brackets is the last letter but one in the word on the left; the 2nd letter is the one preceding it. The 3rd letter is the last letter but one in the word on the right; the 4th is the one preceding it.
7	13	On each line, the right-hand number is obtained by adding together the

PROBLEM No.	SOLUTION	EXPLANATION

first two numbers and subtracing the third number.

$$4 + 3 - 2 = 5$$
$$9 + 5 - 3 = 11$$
$$11 + 7 - 5 = 13$$

| 8 | Q | Starting with C, the 3rd letter of the alphabet, the following letters between the A's correspond to the continuation of the prime numbers: C (3), E (5), G (7), K (11), M (13) and Q, the 17th letter of the alphabet. |

| 9 | 66 and 69 | The sequence continues by using this progression: +3, ×2:
$3(+3) = 6(×2) = 12(+3) = 15(×2) = 30(+3) = 33(×2) = 66(+3) = 69$ |

| 10 | 4 | Number 4 is the identical one. The other three have different patterns. |

| 11 | | The figure should be shaded like this: |

PROBLEM No.	SOLUTION	EXPLANATION

12 6/5

The top half of the right hand domino is obtained by adding together the top halves of the two dominoes preceding it. The bottom half of the domino follows a decreasing progression: 6, 5, 4, 3, 2, 1, 0, 6, 5.

13

The bottom right-hand grid in figure two has an additional black square (bottom right).

14

Figure b is identical to the mosaic when turned 90° anti-clockwise.

15

All the sums are correct except for the last one: $913 - 357 = 556$.

16

A word is to a sentence what a letter is to a word.

17 10

The number is obtained by adding together the three exterior numbers and then subtracting the two interior numbers:
$(8 + 12 + 15) - (11 + 17) = 7$
$(22 + 9 + 8) - (13 + 16) = 10$

18 silk

Silk is the only fibre that has animal origins.

19

5 The line inside the triangle moves clockwise, and the square and circle move anti-clockwise, with the circle always preceding the square.

PROBLEM No.	SOLUTION	EXPLANATION
20	5	The second figure of each pair is reduced by half, and the internal shape becomes exterior and pivots 90°. All the surfaces change colour.

STOP: THIS IS WHERE THE REAL TEST BEGINS. HAVE YOU READ ALL THE INSTRUCTIONS THOROUGHLY?

If everything is O.K. you can begin. If not, return to the beginning of the chapter.

Provide yourself with a pencil and paper to note your answers. You will save yourself time checking them. You must strictly obey the time limit allowed for each test.

Test I

ATTENTION: YOU HAVE 15 MINUTES AND NOT
A MINUTE MORE.

1. How many different 'A's are there?

2. Which figure completes the sequence?

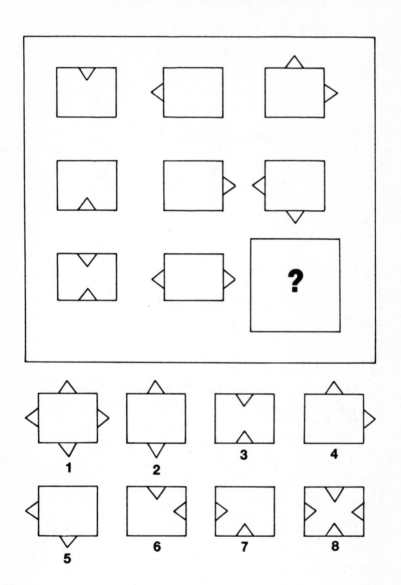

3. Which word completes the sentence?

Controversy is to quarrel as agreement is to . . .

concord, joy, diversity, satisfaction, agony

4. Find the missing number.

326 (20) 432
437 (?) 113

5. Which is the odd word out?

rapier, cutlass, claymore, foil, musket, sabre

6. Which word, when placed in the brackets, forms a different word with each letter(s) that precedes it?

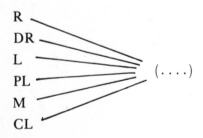

R
DR
L
PL   (. . . .)
M
CL

7. Study this patchwork. How many different patterns are there?

8. What is the hidden card?

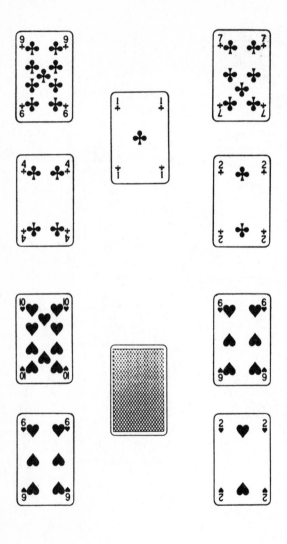

9. Which figure completes the sequence?

A	B
C	D

C	A
D	B

D	C
B	A

?

A	C
D	B

1

B	D
C	A

2

A	D
C	B

3

C	B
D	A

4

B	D
A	C

5

D	C
B	A

6

10. Which figure completes the sequence?

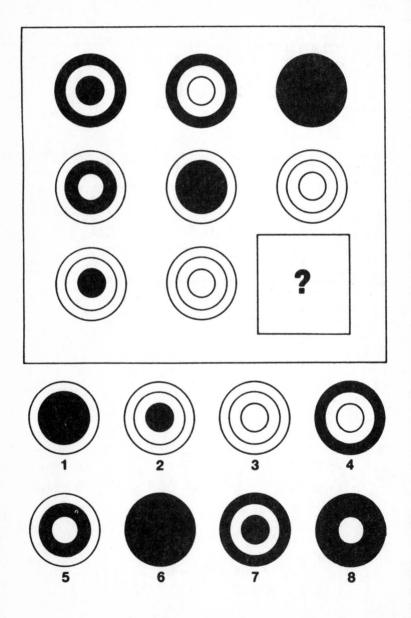

11. Find the missing number.

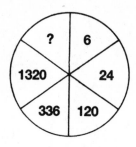

12. What are the missing numbers?

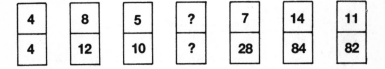

13. Study this shape. With which other shape (a, b, c, d, or e) does it form a rectangle?

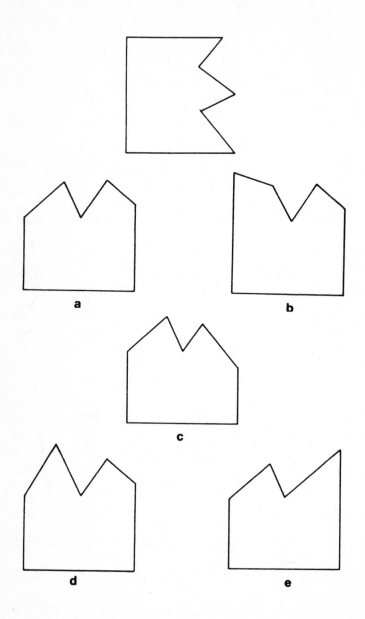

14. Fill in the missing domino.

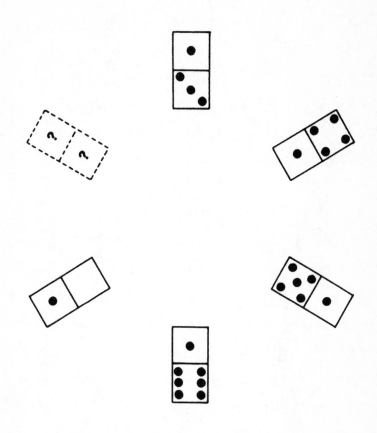

15. Which figure completes the sequence?

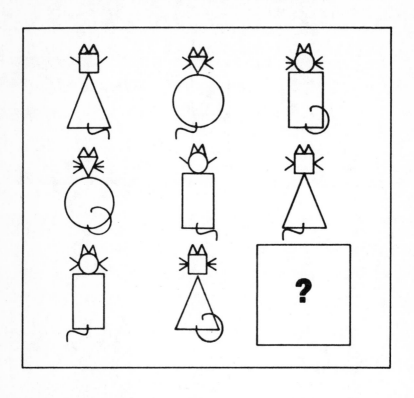

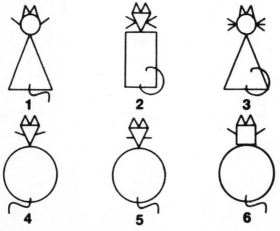

16. Find a word which, when placed in the brackets, forms two different words with the ones either side of it. (*clue:* Aura).

IMP (...) GUN

17. Complete the sequence.

209 (T)   558 (F)   336 (T)   839 (.)

18. Which word goes in the brackets?

HUMP (PUSH) HAST
MIST (....) TONE

19. Find a word which, when placed in the brackets, forms different words with each letter(s) that precedes it.

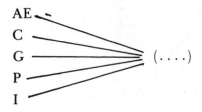

AE
C
G
P
I
(....)

20. Spot the difference between the two pictures.

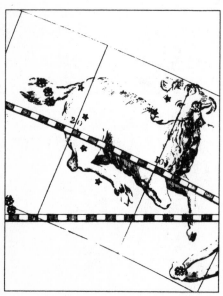

Test II

ATTENTION: YOU HAVE 15 MINUTES AND NOT A MINUTE MORE.

1. All these ships are identical except one. Which one?

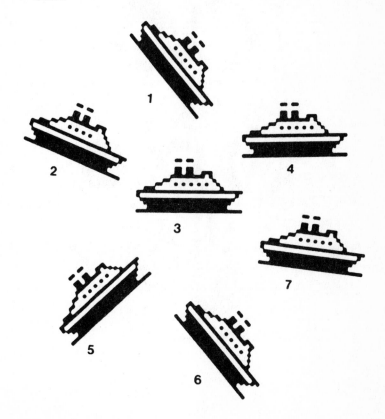

2. Which figure, of the five shown, completes the sequence?

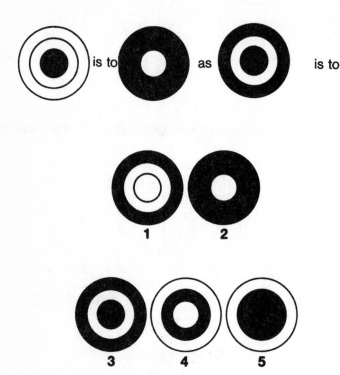

3. Which figure completes the sequence?

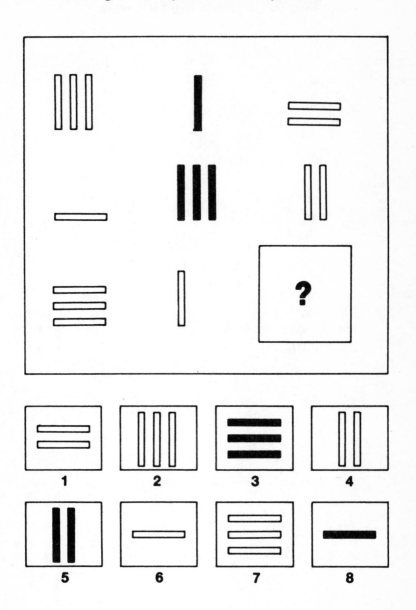

4. **Each dot represents a number or letter that you must find to complete the sequence.**

1A   2D   3I   4P   . .

5. **Fill in the brackets.**

BLACK (BIRD) CAGE
GREEN (. . . . .) HOLD

6. **Which word goes in the brackets?**

HATCH (BACK) DOOR
EGG (. . . . .) FISH

7. **Find a word which, when placed in the brackets, forms two different words with the letters each side.**

GR (. .) TO

8. Which figure completes the sequence?

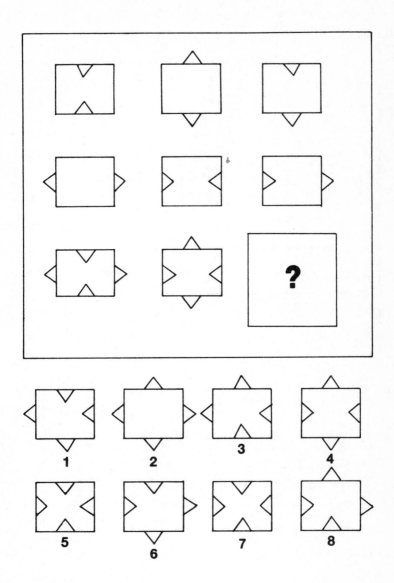

9. Which figure completes the sequence?

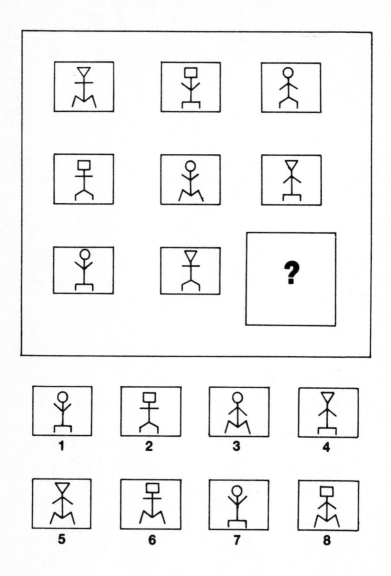

10. What is the hidden card?

11. Find the missing number.

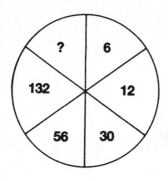

12. Find the missing number.

14	28	10	?
11	15	12	17
25	13	22	16

13. Look at this figure. How many times are shapes a, b and c shown.

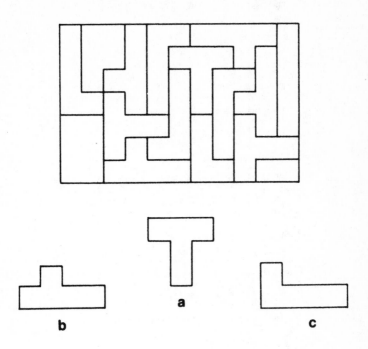

a

b

c

14. How many faces does this shape have?

15. Fill in the missing domino.

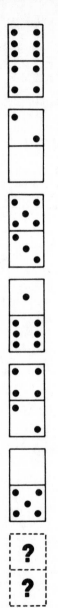

16. Find a word which, when placed in the brackets, forms two different words with the letters each side, and can tell you where someone is.

SL (..) OM

17. Which is the odd word out?

ONACE
ERVLE
INREL
FRYER

18. What word goes in the brackets?

PANTOMINE (CHRISTMAS) CAROL
PARADE (......) EGG

19. Fill in the brackets with a word that forms a different word with each of the preceding letter(s).

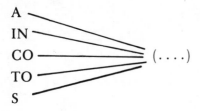

A
IN
CO
TO
S
(....)

20. These two figures are almost identical but for one difference. What is it?

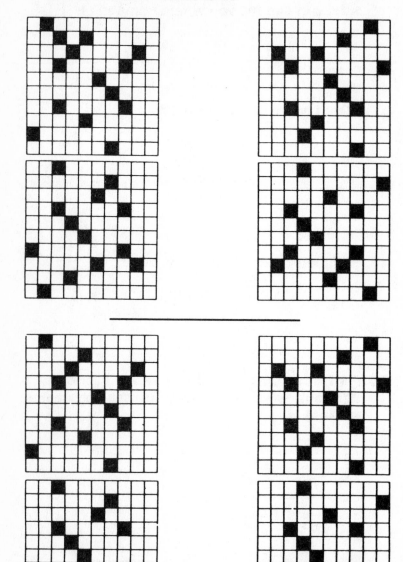

Test III

ATTENTION: YOU HAVE 15 MINUTES ONLY.

1. **How many different shapes are there, not taking size into account?**

2. Which figure completes the sequence?

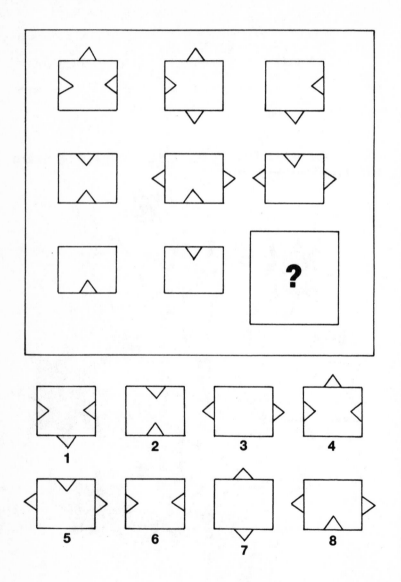

3. **Study this shape. When turned 90° clockwise, which figure does it become; 'a', 'b', 'c' or 'd'?**

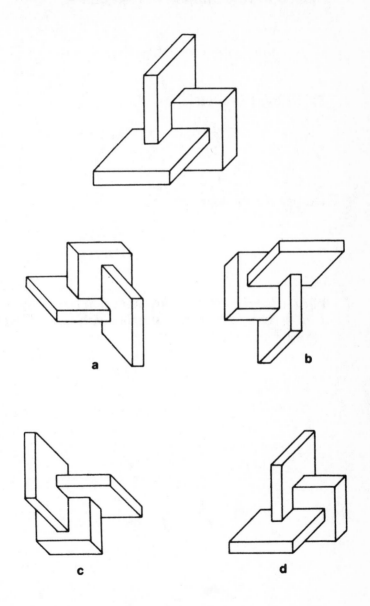

4. **Each dot represents a letter or number that you must find to complete the sequence.**

> M2   R5   U1   B3   E4   UMBER
> R5   M2   E4   A1   B3   . . . . .

5. **Fill in the brackets.**

> MOW (WARN) BARREN
> HAD (. . . .) CUEIST

6. **Complete the second line.**

> DAME (MEAD) MADE
> POSH (. . . .) HOPS

7. **Find a word which, when placed in the brackets, forms two different words with the letters either side.**

> UR (. . .) KER

8. Which figure completes the sequence?

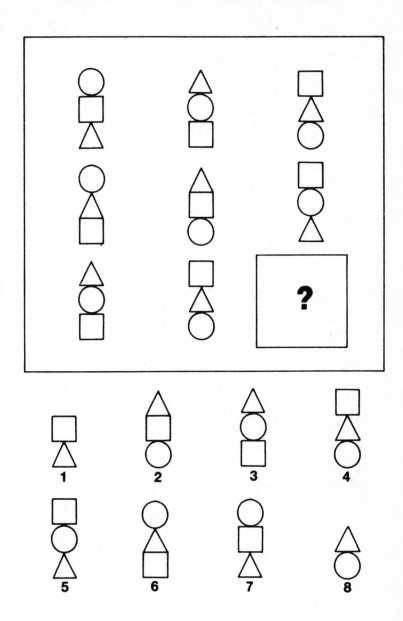

9. What are the hidden cards?

10. Find the missing number.

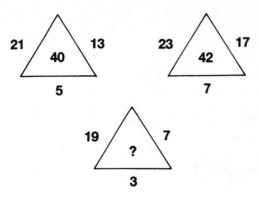

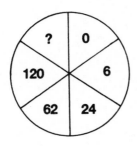

11. Find the missing number.

12. How many cats are there in this drawing?

13. Which figure completes the sequence?

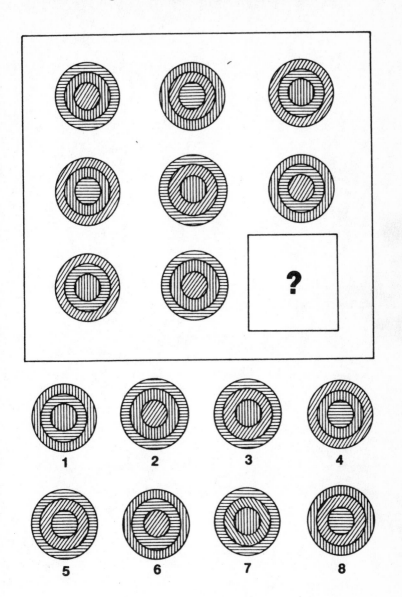

14. Fill in the missing domino.

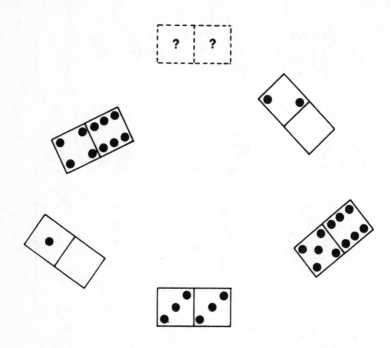

15. Which figure completes the sequence?

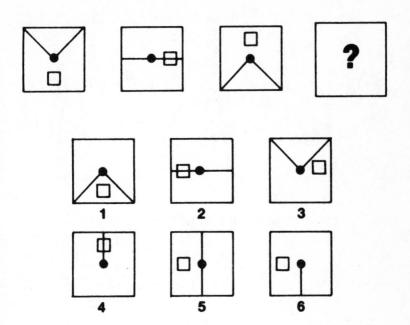

16. Find a word which, when placed in the brackets, forms two different words with the letters each side of it.

BA (. . .) US

17. The dot represents a number that you must find to complete the sequence.

CHEF	JOCKEY	SWEEP	COOK
4	6	5	.

18. What word goes in the brackets?

STEAL (LATER) TRIAL
FRAUD (. . . . .) ALARM

19. Fill in the brackets to form a different word with each preceding letter(s).

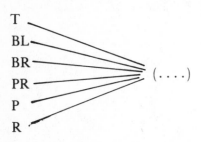

T
BL
BR
PR
P
R

(. . . .)

20. Spot the difference between these two nearly identical figures.

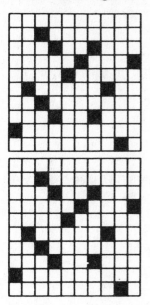

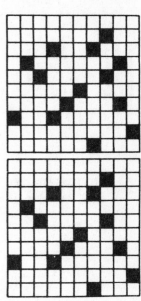

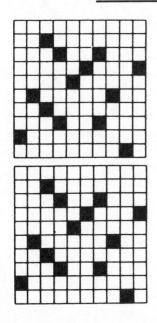

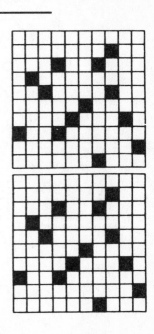

Test IV

ATTENTION: YOU HAVE ONLY 15 MINUTES TO DO THIS TEST.

1. On this map of Spain, one area has been blacked out. Which of the three figures is it?

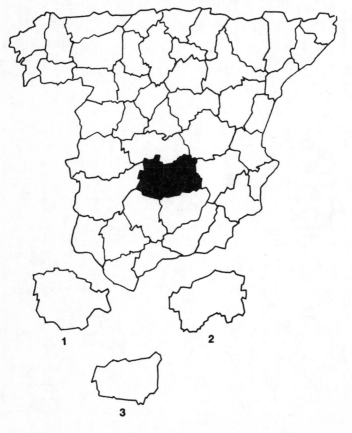

2. Which figure completes the sequence?

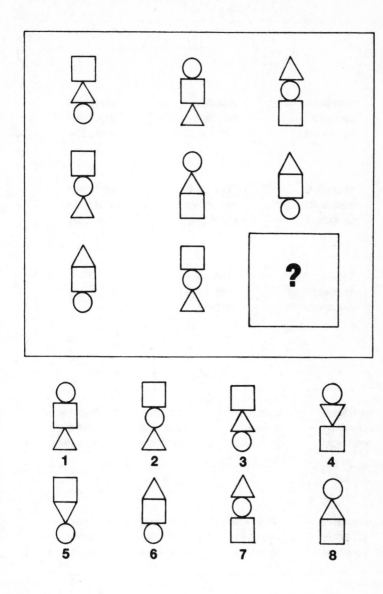

3. Which figure completes the sequence?

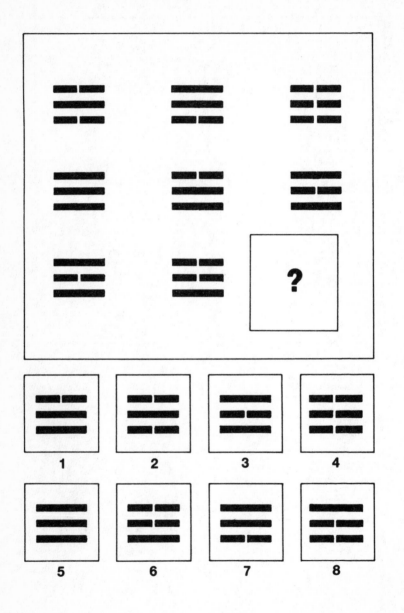

4. Which word completes the sentence?

'An oasis is to the desert what an island is ...'.

to the earth, to the sky, to paradise, to hell, to a fisherman, to the sea.

5. Find the missing number.

38 (82) 3
6 (?) 47

6. Which is the odd one out?

circle,   triangle,   rectangle
square,   cube,   rhombus

7. Fill in the brackets with a word that forms a different word with each preceding letter(s).

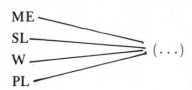

ME
SL
W
PL
(...)

8. How many right way up, and how many upside down cable cars are there?

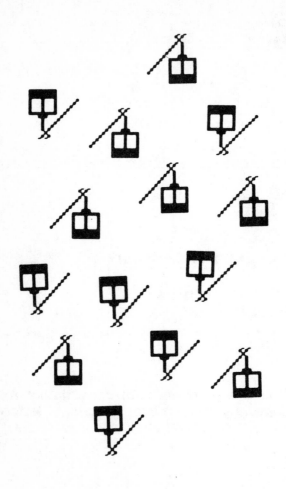

9. Fill in the missing domino.

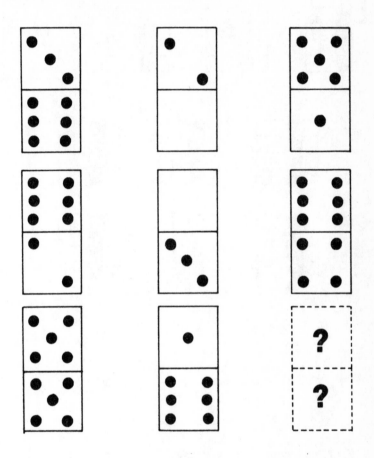

10. Which figure completes the sequence?

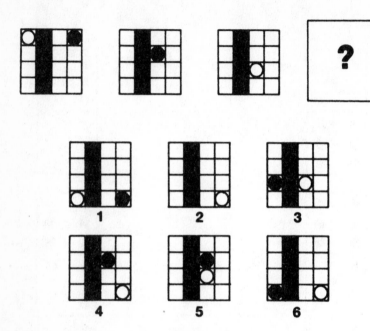

11. Find the missing numbers.

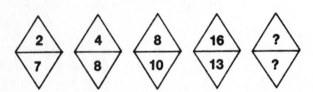

12. Find the missing number.

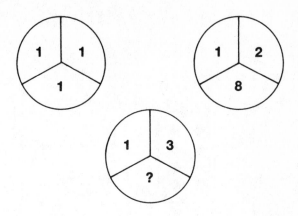

13. Look at these bars for 15 seconds. Then group together the ones of the same length.

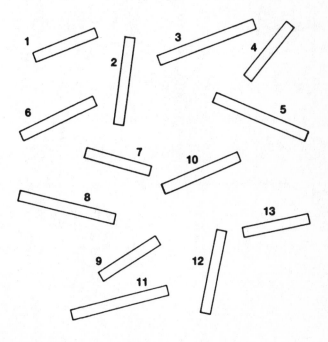

14. What is the missing card?

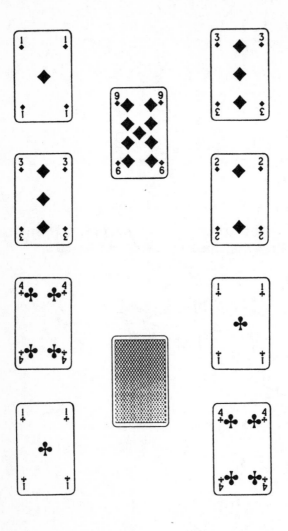

15. Which figure completes the sequence?

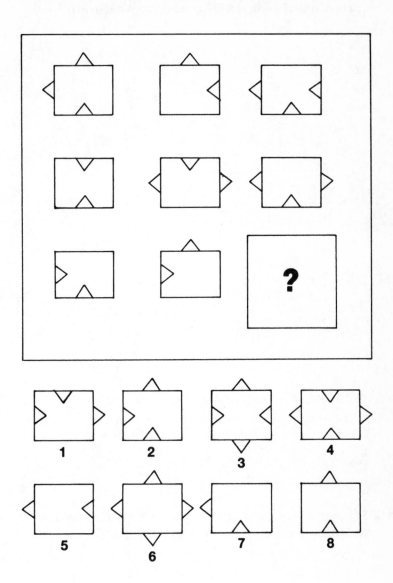

16. Fill in the brackets with a word that forms a different word with each preceding letter(s).

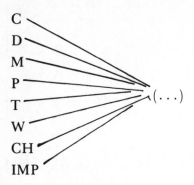

C
D
M
P
T
W
CH
IMP

(. . .)

17. Fill in the brackets.

SHOE (HORSE) RADISH
LILY (. . . . .) MOTH

18. What word goes in the brackets?

FINGER (GRAFT) SATSUMA
RUSSET (. . . . .) BATHING

19. Fill in the brackets with a word that forms two different words with the letters each side.

TO (. . . .) EN

20. Spot the difference between these two nearly
identical pictures.

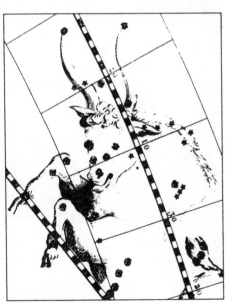

Solutions

Each correct answer is worth one point. Check your answers with the following solutions and add up your points test by test.

Test I

PROBLEM No.	SOLUTION	EXPLANATION
1	10	There are 15 A's in the drawing, and 10 are of a different shape.
2	1	The bottom figure of each column is obtained by adding together the triangles in the two preceding figures.
3	concord	Synonymous with agreement, as quarrel is with controversy.
4	19	The number in brackets is obtained by adding together all the numbers outside the brackets: $3 + 2 + 6 + 4 + 3 + 2 = 20$ $4 + 3 + 7 + 1 + 1 + 3 = 19$
5	musket	A gun, the rest are swords.
6	over	which forms the words: rover, drover, lover, plover, mother, clover.

PROBLEM No.	SOLUTION	EXPLANATION
7	9	There are nine different patterns on the patch-work.
8	Ace of Hearts	The cards are arranged in two groups of five. The top group is Clubs, the bottom group is Hearts. In each of the groups, the value of the centre card is obtained by dividing the difference between the values of the two highest value cards by the difference between the values of the two lowest value cards:

Thus: $\dfrac{(9-7)}{(4-2)} = \dfrac{2}{2} = 1 =$ Ace of Clubs

and: $\dfrac{(10-6)}{(6-2)} = \dfrac{4}{4} = 1 =$ Ace of Hearts

9	5	Each letter moves one space clockwise each time.
10	1	On each line the right hand figure is obtained by changing the colour of the middle ring, and alternating the colour of the inner circle.
11	2184	The sequence is prime numbers. Each number is obtained by taking the prime number, cubing

PROBLEM No.	SOLUTION	EXPLANATION

it, and then subtracting its own value from the result:
$2^3 - 2 = 6$, $3^3 - 3 = 24$, $5^3 - 5 = 120$, $7^3 - 7 = 336$, $11^3 - 11 = 1320$, $13^3 - 13 = 2184$.

12

10

30

In the top square, the equation to follow is $\times 2$, -3: $4 (\times 2 =)$ 8, $(-3 =)$ 5, $(\times 2 =)$ 10, $(-3 =)$ 7, etc. In the bottom square, the equation to follow is $\times 3$, -2: $4 (\times 3 =)$ 12, $(-2 =)$ 10, $(\times 3 =)$ 30, $(-2 =)$ 28, etc.

13

a

Figure 'a' forms a perfect rectangle when placed together with the top figure.

14   Double One

The number 1 is on each domino, alternating between exterior and interior. Starting with the number three on the top domino, the progression is 3, 4, 5, 6, 0, 1, also alternating from interior to exterior.

15   5

The body and heads of the cats are made up of three shapes; the square, circle and triangle. These shapes change their order on each line. The cat's tail changes side from left to right, then it is curled up on itself. The whiskers have 2, 3 or 4 hairs.

PROBLEM No.	SOLUTION	EXPLANATION
16	air	A synonym of the word aura, which forms the words impair and air-gun.
17	E	The letter that follows each number is the first letter of that number when it is written out in full. T for two hundred and nine, F for five hundred and fifty eight, T for three hundred and thirty six and E for eight hundred and thirty nine.
18	tint	The first two letters of the word in brackets are the fourth and second letters of the left hand word. The last two letters of the word in brackets are the third and first letters of the right hand word.
19	rate	Which forms the words: aerate, crate, grate, prate and irate.
20		In the bottom picture, the ram's left antler is missing.

Test II

PROBLEM No.	SOLUTION	EXPLANATION
1	2	The second ship only has four portholes. All the others have five.
2	4	The colours are reversed on the second figure of each pair.
3	5	On each line, there are three different figures in a changing order. One of these figures is black. The white figures alternate between being vertical and horizontal.
4	5Y	The sequence is that of whole numbers; 1, 2, 3, 4, 5. The letter that follows this number is obtained by squaring the number, and the result gives you the letter's position in the alphabet. i.e. $5^2 = 25$. Y = 25th letter of the alphabet. $1^2 = 1 = $ A, 1st letter $2^2 = 4 = $ D, 4th letter $3^2 = 9 = $ I, 9th letter $4^2 = 16 = $ P, 16th letter $5^2 = 25 = $ Y, 25th letter
5	house	Bird can follow black and go before cage. House can follow green and go before hold.

PROBLEM No.	SOLUTION	EXPLANATION
6	shell	Back can follow Hatch and go before Door. Shell can follow Egg and go before Fish.
7	in	Which forms the words grin and into.
8	$\bar{6}$	The bottom figure of each column is obtained by superimposing the preceding two.
9	8	On each line, the head is represented by one of these three shapes: circle, triangle or square. The arms and knees are up once, down once and horizontal once.
10	Ace of Diamonds	On the two vertical lines, there are the four suits: Hearts, Clubs, Spades and Diamonds. In each group of five cards (Joker included) the diagonals add up to the same amount. Top group: $10 + 2 = 7 + 5 = 12$ Lower group: $8 + (1) = 3 + 6 = 9$
11	182	The sequence is that of prime numbers. Each number in the circle represents a prime number and its square, added together:

PROBLEM No.	SOLUTION	EXPLANATION
		$2 + 2^2 = 6, 3 + 3^2 = 12,$ $5 + 5^2 = 30, 7 + 7^2 = 56,$ $11 + 11^2 = 132,$ $13 + 13^2 = 182.$
12	33	Starting from the left, the bottom or top numbers of each column are obtained by adding together the two numbers that precede it: $25 = 14 + 11$ $28 = 15 + 13$ $22 = 10 + 12$ $(33) = 17 + 16$
13	3, 4, 4	Shape 'a' is shown three times. Shapes 'b' and 'c' are shown four times.
14	5	The figure has five sides. Only two are visible.
15	Three/One	Starting with the six on the top domino, the numbers simply decrease, with one number being missed out between each half of the dominoes and between the dominoes themselves. 6 (5) 4 [3] 2 (1) 0 [6] 5 (4) 3 [2] 1 (0) 6 [5] 4 (3) 2 [1] 0 (6) 5 [4] 3 (2) 1
16	at	Which forms the words slat and atom.

PROBLEM No.	SOLUTION	EXPLANATION
17	ERVLE	An anagram of lever. The others are anagrams of boats: canoe, liner, ferry.
18	easter	Christmas is connected with pantomime and carol. Easter is connected with parade and egg.
19	ward	Which forms the words: award, inward, coward, toward and sword.
20		In the second figure, a black square is missing at the top left.

Test III

PROBLEM No.	SOLUTION	EXPLANATION
1	9	Out of the 29 stars in the picture, only nine have a different shape, regardless of size.
2	2	On each line, the right hand figure is obtained by superimposing the two preceding it. Identical shapes cancel each other out.
3	c	When turned 90° clockwise, the figure becomes figure 'c'.
4	amber	The number after each letter gives its position in the word that follows.
5	duet	The first letter of the words in brackets is the last letter of the word to the left of it. The second, third and fourth letters are the second, third and sixth letters of the word to the right of it.
6	shop	Mead is an anagram of Dame and Made. Shop is an anagram of Posh and Hops.
7	ban	Which forms the words: urban and banker.

PROBLEM No.	SOLUTION	EXPLANATION

8 7 On each line, the same three shapes are present, but in a different order each time.

9   Nine   and   Two
    of Clubs   of Hearts

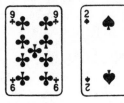

On each line, the right hand card is the same suit as the two preceding it. The number on the right hand card is obtained by dividing the number on the first card by the number on the second:
$4 \div 2 = 2$, $6 \div 2 = 3$,
$9 \div 1 = 9$, $10 \div 5 = 2$.

10   19

7 The number at the centre of the triangle is obtained each time by subtracting the number on the right hand side from the number on the left hand side and multiplying the result by the base:
$(21 - 13) \times 5 = 40$,
$(23 - 17) \times 7 = 42$,
$(19 - 7) \times 3 = 36$.

11   210

Taking whole numbers from 1 to 6, the numbers in the circle are obtained by cubing each number, and then subtracting itself from the result:
$1^3 - 1 = 0$, $2^3 - 2 = 6$,
$3^3 - 3 = 24$, $4^3 - 4 = 62$,
$5^3 - 5 = 120$,
$6^3 - 6 = 210$.

12   22

There are 22 cats in the picture.

PROBLEM No.	SOLUTION	EXPLANATION
13		8 Each figure is made up of three patterns: vertical, horizontal and diagonal stripes. These three patterns appear on each line, but in a different order.
14	Five/Two	Moving anti-clockwise from the domino 6/4, the numbers on one half of the domino change by two each time: 6 (0) 1 (2) 3 (4) 5 (6) 0 (1) 2. On the other half the number changes by three: 4 (5/6) 0 (1/2) 3 (4/5) 6 (0/1) 2 (3/4) 5.
15	6	The right hand line moves 45° clockwise each time; the left hand line moves 45° anti-clockwise. The square moves 90° anti-clockwise each time.
16	lot	Which forms the words: balot and lotus.
17	4	The number under each word corresponds to the amount of letters in that word.
18	mural	The first and last letters of the word in brackets are the last and second letters of the word to the right of it. The second, third and fourth letters are the fourth, second and third letters of the word to the left.

PROBLEM No.	SOLUTION	EXPLANATION
19	each	Which forms the words: teach, bleach, breach, preach, peach and reach.
20		A black square is missing in the top right hand grid of the second figure.

Test IV

PROBLEM No.	SOLUTION	EXPLANATION
1		Figure 2 is the missing area.
2	8	Each line and each figure is made up of the same three shapes changing their order; square, circle and triangle.
3	5	The right hand figure on each line is obtained by taking the top line of the first figure, changing the middle line from the first two figures, and leaving the bottom line as it is.
4	sea	'An oasis is to the desert what an island is to the sea.'
5	106	The number in brackets is obtained by adding together the numbers either side and multiplying by 2: $38 + 3 = 41 \times 2 = 82$ $6 + 47 = 53 \times 2 = 106$
6	cube	A cube is the only shape with a volume amongst the other flat shapes.
7	ant	Which forms the words: meant, slant, want and plant.
8	7	There are 14 cable cars. Seven are the right way up and seven upside down.

PROBLEM No.	SOLUTION	EXPLANATION
9	Six/Zero	On each line, the top half of the right hand domino is obtained by adding together the top halves of the two dominoes preceding it. The bottom halves of the dominoes follow the sequence: 6, 0, 1, 2, 3, 4, 5, 6, 0.
10	6	The white circle moves one place diagonally from left to right, top to bottom. The black circle moves one place diagonally from right to left, top to bottom.
11	32 17	The top number of each figure is obtained by multiplying the preceding number by 2. At the bottom, there is an increasing gap of one number each time; $7(+1=)$ $8(+2=)$ $10(+3=)$ 13, etc.
12	27	In each circle, the bottom number is equal to the cube of the two top numbers multiplied together: $(1 \times 1)^3 = 1$, $(1 \times 2)^3 = 8$, $(1 \times 3)^3 = 27$.
13		There are three different lengths, and the groups are: (1, 4, 7, 9, 13), (2, 6, 10, 12), (3, 5, 8, 11).

PROBLEM No.	SOLUTION	EXPLANATION
14	Ten of Clubs	There are two groups of cards, 5 Diamonds and 5 Clubs. In each group, the number of the centre card is equal to the other four cards added up: $1 + 3 + 3 + 2 = 9$ $4 + 1 + 1 + 4 = 10$
15	8	On each line, the right hand figure is obtained by superimposing the two preceding it. Identical triangles cancel each other out.
16	art	Which forms the words: cart, dart, mart, part, tart, wart, chart and impart.
17	tiger	Horse goes in front of both shoe and radish. Tiger goes in front of both lily and moth.
18	start	The first, second and fourth letters of the words in brackets are the fourth, last and first letters of the word to the left of it; the third and last letters are the second and third letters of the word to the right.
19	ward	Which forms the words: toward and warden.
20		In the second picture, a star is missing in the bottom right hand corner.

FUNCTION	Test I	Test II	Test III	Test IV	
Logic Question Nos.	2, 8, 9, 10, 14, 15	2, 3, 8, 9, 10 15	2, 8, 9, 13, 14, 15	2, 3, 9, 10, 14, 15	Total questions: 24 Correct answers:
Perception Question Nos.	1, 7, 13, 20	1, 13, 14, 20	1, 3, 12, 10	1, 8, 13, 20	Total questions: 16 Correct answers:
Language Question Nos.	3, 5, 6, 16, 18, 19	5, 6, 7, 16, 17, 18, 19	5, 6, 7, 16 18, 19	4, 6, 7, 16, 17, 18, 19	Total questions: 26 Correct answers:
Numeracy Question Nos.	4, 11, 12, 17	4, 11, 12	4, 10, 11, 17	5, 11, 12	Total questions: 14 Correct answers:
	TOTAL QUESTIONS 40 Correct answers . . .		TOTAL QUESTIONS 40 Correct answers . . .		

Your results

Write your different scores into the table on the previous page. In this way you will have a more detailed picture of your results.

How to interpret your results

You can interpret your results in two ways:

— Taken as a whole, by measuring your I.Q. which allows you to evaluate your level of intelligence and compare yourself in relation to others;

— By taking each area individually, which allows you to see your strongest and weakest points in the different intellectual levels.

What is your intelligence quotient?

You now have everything you need to calculate your I.Q.
Refer to the following table.

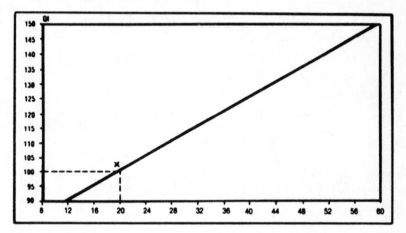

This table allows you to transform your score into an I.Q.
To do this you must:

• Add up all the correct answers you obtained in tests 1 and 2;

• Mark this number on the horizontal line of the table;

• Draw a perpendicular up to the diagonal line on the table. This is point X, and is vertically above 20 in the example shown.

• Draw a horizontal from point X to the vertical line on the table. This gives you your I.Q.

• Do the same thing with the answers you obtained in tests 3 and 4 to give you a second I.Q. evaluation.

These two evaluations, which often vary, show you how your intellectual output and your performance can change from one moment to the next during one hour of solid 'work'.

Add your two scores together and divide by two to give you a more realistic indication of your true I.Q.

How you compare

Finally, here is a table devised by Wechsler that you can use to compare your intelligence level with the rest of the population.

I.Q.	Intelligence Level	Percentage of population
130 and above	Very high	2.2%
120 - 129	High	6.7%
110 - 119	Above average	16.1%
90 - 109	Average	50 %
80 - 89	Below average	16.1%
70 - 79	Low	6.7%
60 or below	Deficient	2.2%

• **Between 90 and 110** — You have an average I.Q. Your intelligence is suited to everyday life, and you are easily able to overcome the daily problems life presents.

• **Between 110 and 120** — You are above average; you have an ability to solve problems quickly and efficiently, occasionally showing flashes of brilliance.

• **Between 120 and 130** — You are either particularly on form intellectually at the moment, or very gifted at resolving the sort of problems posed by these tests. A more detailed assessment might be desirable to confirm your performance.

- **Less than 90 and more than 130** — (less than 20 correct answers or more than 42 in two tests). You fall into the categories of 'inferior' and 'highly superior'. The probability that you are one or the other is extremely small. It might be better to admit that this sort of test is not really suitable for evaluating your degree of intelligence.

Taking each area separately

- You are 'weak' in a particular area if you have scored less than a quarter correct answers: less than six for 'logic', less than four for 'perception', less than six for 'language' and less than three for 'numeracy'.

- Compare your results for 'language' and 'numeracy'. If your 'language' results are better, you find it easier to reason from the general to the particular, your powers of deduction are good. However, if your performance in 'numeracy' is better, you have an aptitude for induction, reasoning from the particular to the general.
  This is for your interest only, since it is very difficult, if not impossible, to separate induction and deduction.

- Compare your results in 'logic' and 'perception' to those in 'language' and 'numeracy'.
  A better performance in the first two suggests a more 'visual' form of intelligence. You find it easy to think in images; you have a good perception of shapes.
  However, better results in the second two areas; 'language' and 'numeracy' signals towards a more 'conceptual' form of intelligence. You find it easier to think in words, and have a good understanding of symbols.

SHORT PROGRAMME

The short programme is normally completed over five days. It has been devised to very quickly 'put your mind in gear' if you have scholastic or professional tests coming up.

You can, if necessary, do the programme in one day, but if you complete it in five days you will absorb the problems and the methods of resolving them much better.

The first four days each deal with a particular 'subject'; perception, language, logic and numbers.

In each subject there are ten problems, and you have eight minutes to mentally resolve them.

The fifith day is a summary of all the previous subjects put together; five problems on each subject making 20 problems in total, and you have 15 minutes to find the solution.

Every day you can establish your score in one particular subject and compare it to your previous performance. (see Assess Yourself).

A few words of advice

You need 15 minutes a day to do these exercises. Make sure you do them under good conditions. Choose a time of day when you won't be disturbed, and a nice quiet area. Provide yourself with a pen and paper (solely to write your answers), disconnect your telephone and settle down comfortably. Use an alarm clock or stopwatch to prevent you from worrying about the time. For more advice, return to the previous chapter.

Day One
Perception

ATTENTION: YOU HAVE ONLY 8 MINUTES TO
SOLVE 10 PROBLEMS.

1. How many different 'ones' are there?

2. Spot the difference between these two nearly identical pictures.

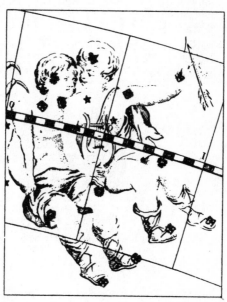

3. Which of the three shown below does this figure become when rotated 180° clockwise?

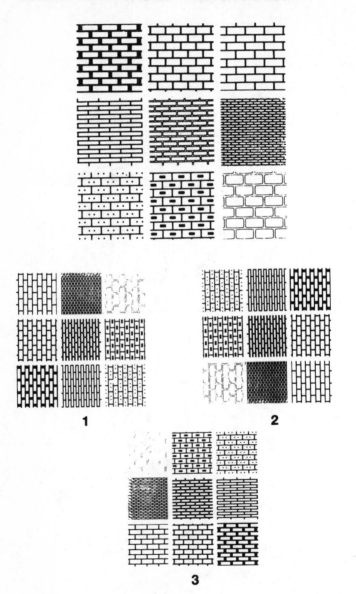

1

2

3

4. Look at this shape. It has been made by folding one of the three figures below — which one?

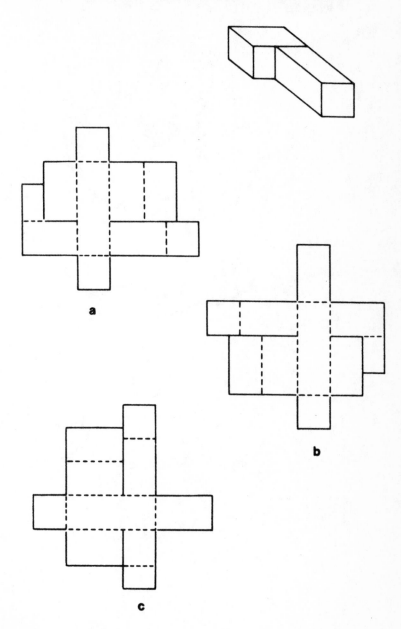

a

b

c

5. On this map of France, one of the areas has been shaded in. Which shape, 1, 2, or 3 completes the map?

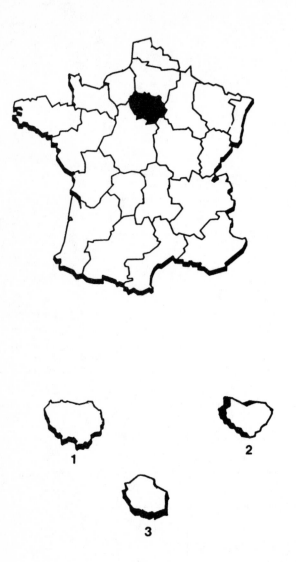

1

2

3

6. **All of these letters are identical, other than in size, except one. Which one?**

7. **Spot the difference between these two nearly identical pictures.**

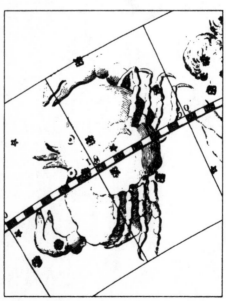

8. All these symbols are different, except two. Which ones?

9. How many sides does this solid have?

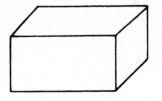

10. Study this chessboard for 30 seconds. Memorise the position of each playing piece. Then cover it up and . . .

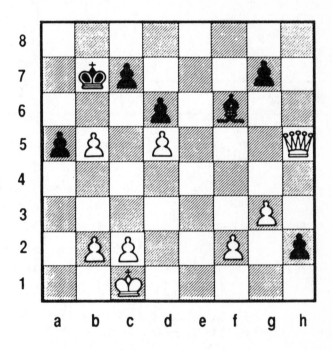

try to remember the position of the black Bishop.

Perception: solutions

PROBLEM	SOLUTION
1	Eleven of the fifteen 'ones' are different.
2	A 'zero' is missing in the second picture just above the centre line on the right hand side.
3	When the figure is rotated 180° clockwise, it becomes the figure 3.
4	The shape has been made from figure b.
5	Figure 'I' completes the map of France.
6	The only letter that is not identical is the 'a', third from the left on the bottom line.
7	A star is missing in the second picture, under the line on the right hand side.
8	The only identical pair is the symbol on the top left, and the one on the extreme right on the fourth line. On the last line, the middle symbol has a smaller angle than the other two.
9	The shape has six sides.
10	The position of the black Bishop, is remembered by memorising the coordinates, f6.

Day Two
Language

ATTENTION: YOU HAVE 8 MINUTES TO SOLVE
10 PROBLEMS.

---

1. **Find a word to fill the brackets which forms a different word with each of the preceding letters.**

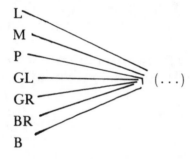

L
M
P
GL
GR
BR
B

(...)

2. **What word goes in the brackets?**

METAL ROD (POKER) CARD GAME
CASH REGISTER (....) PLOUGH

3. **Fill in the brackets on the second line.**

SELECT (PICK) TOOL
CUT BACK (.....) FRUIT

4. **Find a word which, when placed in the brackets, forms two different words with the letters either side of it.**

AB (...) LESS

5. **Find a word which, when placed in the brackets, forms two different words with the letters either side of it.**

DE (. . . .) IAL

6. **Which is the odd one out?**

EACHTHE
URCAGO
LAJKAC
BARNOC

7. **What word goes in the brackets?**

MARGIN (ANGER) FLAMES
RESIST (. . . . .) MISERY

8. **Fill in the brackets with a word that forms a different word with each preceding letter(s).**

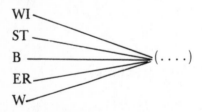

WI
ST
B
ER
W
(. . . .)

9. **Which word completes the sentence?**

'A pair of compasses are to circumference as a set square is to . . .'.

length, a right angle, height, surface area.

10. Which is the odd one out?

gull, heron, swan, duck, goose.

Language: solutions

PROBLEM No.	SOLUTION	EXPLANATION
1	ass	Which forms the words: lass, mass, pass, glass, grass, brass and bass.
2	till	It means the same as both words outside the brackets.
3	prune	It means the same as both words outside the brackets.
4	use	Which forms the words: abuse and useless.
5	part	Which forms the words: depart and partial.
6	BARNOC = CARBON	The rest are anagrams of animals: cheetah, cougar, jackal.
7	stirs	The first and fourth letters of the word in brackets are the third and fifth letters of the word to the right of it. The second, third and fifth letters are the last, fourth and third letters of the word to the left.
8	ring	Which forms the words: wiring, string, bring, erring and wring.

PROBLEM No.	SOLUTION	EXPLANATION
9	right angle	Compasses draw the circumference, a set square is used to draw right angles.
10	heron	A heron is a wader bird, all the others have webbed-feet.

Day Three
Logic

ATTENTION: YOU HAVE 8 MINUTES TO SOLVE
10 PROBLEMS.

1. Which figure completes the sequence?

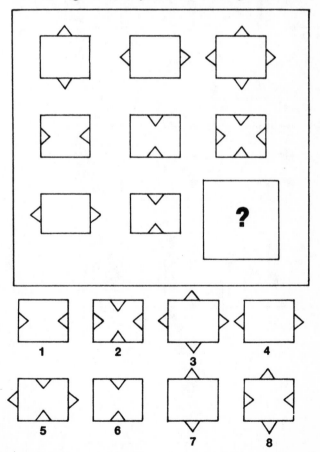

2. What are the hidden cards?

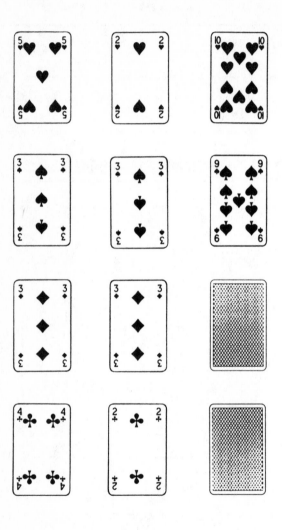

3. **Which figure, of the six shown below, completes the sequence?**

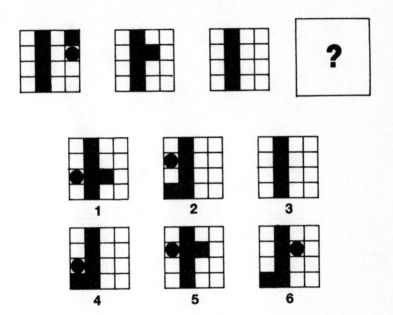

4. Which of these figures is the odd one out?

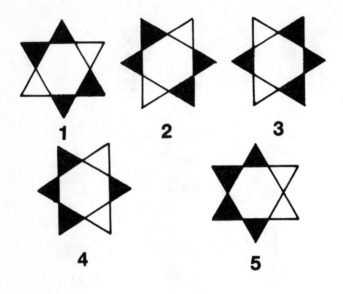

5. Fill in the missing domino.

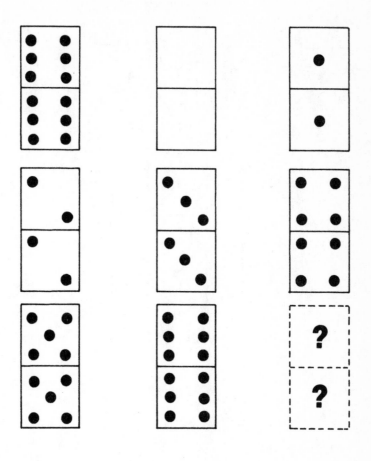

6. Which figure, of the six shown, completes the sequence?

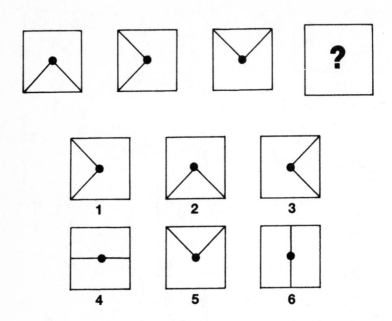

7. Which figure completes the sequence?

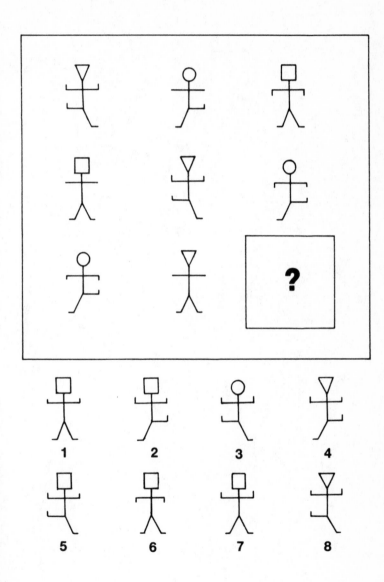

8. Fill in the missing domino.

9. Which figure completes the sequence?

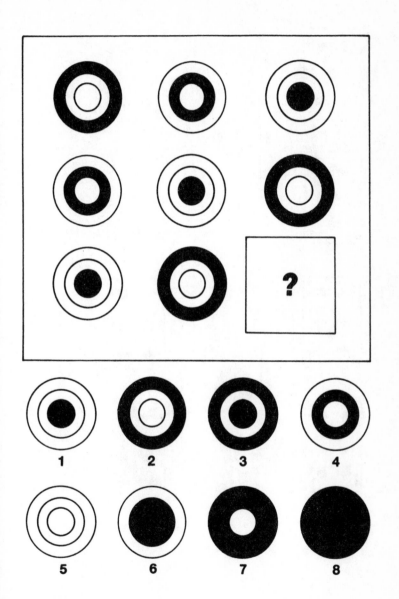

10. What is the hidden card?

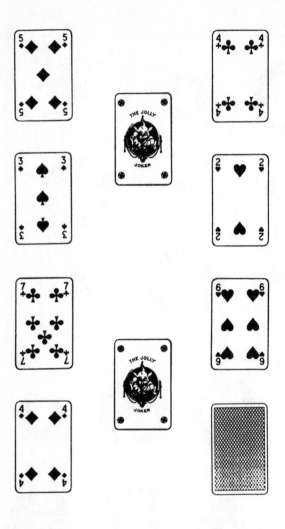

Logic: solutions

PROBLEM No.	SOLUTION	EXPLANATION
1	5	On each line, the right hand figure is obtained by superimposing the two preceding figures.
2	Nine of Diamonds	On each line, the suit of the right hand card is determined by the two preceding cards.
	Eight of Clubs	The number on the card is obtained by multiplying together the value of the two cards preceding it: $5 \times 2 = 10$, $3 \times 3 = 9$, $3 \times 3 = 9$ and $4 \times 2 = 8$.
3	2	The square moves diagonally one place each time from right to left. The circle moves horizontally from right to left.
4	5	Numbers 1 and 2, and 3 and 4 are identical pairs symmetrically.
5	Double zero	Starting with the double six at the top left, and working from left to right, the dominoes go up in doubles.

PROBLEM No.	SOLUTION	EXPLANATION
6		3 The two lines move 90° clockwise each time.
7	5	On each line, the characters heads are represented alternately by three shapes; (triangle, circle and square). The hands alternate between being up, down and straight across. The feet are either both down, left one up or right one up.
8	Three/Zero	Working clockwise, the exterior halves progress, missing out one number each time. The interior halves always add up to five with their opposite domino.
9	4	On each line, the central circle and each of the rings is black once.

PROBLEM No.	SOLUTION	EXPLANATION

10   Three of Spades

The cards are divided into two groups of five. In each group, all the suits are represented, therefore the hidden card must be a Spade. In each group, the diagonal cards must add up to the same number:

1st group:
$5 + 2 = 4 + 3 = 7$.

2nd group:
$7 + 3 = 6 + 4 = 10$.

Day Four
Numbers

ATTENTION: YOU HAVE 8 MINUTES TO SOLVE 10 PROBLEMS.

1. Find the missing number.

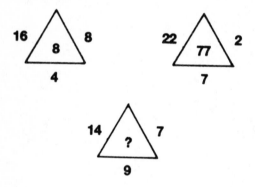

2. Find the missing number.

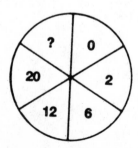

3. What are the missing numbers?

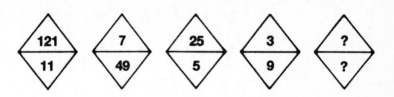

4. What is the missing number?

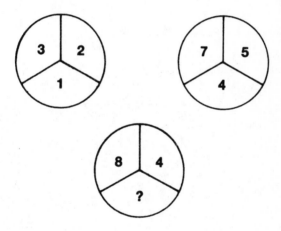

5. Find the missing number.

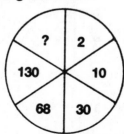

6. Find the missing numbers.

1	1	2	4	8	64	?
2	3	5	7	11	13	?

7. Find the missing number.

47 (81) 38
55 (?) 48

8. Find the missing number.

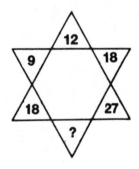

9. Find the missing number.

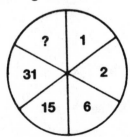

10. Find the missing number.

7	1	2	4
5	4	3	3
11	3	?	7

Numbers: solutions

PROBLEM No.	SOLUTION	EXPLANATION

1

In each triangle, the centre number is obtained by dividing the two side numbers and multiplying the result by the base:
$(16/8) \times 4 = 8,$
$(22/2) \times 7 = 77,$
$(14/7) \times 9 = 18.$

2   30

Using whole numbers from one to six, the numbers are obtained by squaring, and then subtracting itself. i.e.
$1^2 - 1 = 0, 2^2 - 2 = 2,$
$3^2 - 3 = 6, 4^2 - 4 = 12,$
$5^2 - 5 = 20, 6^2 - 6 = 30.$

3

Working from right to left, one half of each diamond is a sequence of prime numbers, alternating between bottom and top. The other halves work in the same way, this time with the prime numbers being squared each time.

4

In each circle, the bottom number is obtained by subtracting the right hand number from the left hand number, and squaring the result:
$3 - 2 = 1^2 = 1$
$7 - 5 = 2^2 = 4$
$8 - 4 = 4^2 = 16$

5   222

The sequence is whole numbers: 1, 2, 3, 4, 5, 6. Each

PROBLEM No.	SOLUTION	EXPLANATION

| | | number in the circle is obtained by cubing a whole number and then adding itself: |

$1^3 + 1 = 2, 2^3 + 2 = 10,$
$3^3 + 3 = 30, 4^3 + 4 = 68,$
$5^3 + 5 = 130, 6^3 + 6 = 222.$

6   **128** / **17**   In the top square the sequence is $(^2)$, $\times 2$:

1 $(^2=)$ 1 $(\times 2=)$ 2 $(^2=)$ 4 $(\times 2=)$ 8 $(^2=)$ 64 $(\times 2=)$ 128.

In the bottom square the sequence is of prime numbers 2, 3, 5, 7, 11, 13, 17.

7   49   The number in brackets is obtained by subtracting the right hand number from the left, and squaring the result:

$(47 - 38 = 9 \, (^2) = 81$
$(55 - 48 = 7 \, (^2) = 49$

8   24   All opposite numbers always add up to 36.

9   56   Each number is obtained by adding 1, 2, 3, 4, 5 squared, to the preceding number:

$\quad 1 \qquad\qquad 1$
$\quad 1 + 1^2 = \quad 2$
$\quad 2 + 2^2 = \quad 6$
$\quad 6 + 3^2 = 15$
$\quad 15 + 4^2 = 31$
$\quad 31 + 5^2 = 56$

10   2   On each line, the third number is equal to the two preceding numbers, divided by the following number:

$7 + 1 = 8/4 = 2$
$5 + 4 = 9/3 = 3$
$11 + 3 = 14/7 = 2$

Day Five: a recap

ATTENTION: YOU HAVE 15 MINUTES TO SOLVE 20 PROBLEMS.

1. Study this picture carefully. Which is the missing piece?

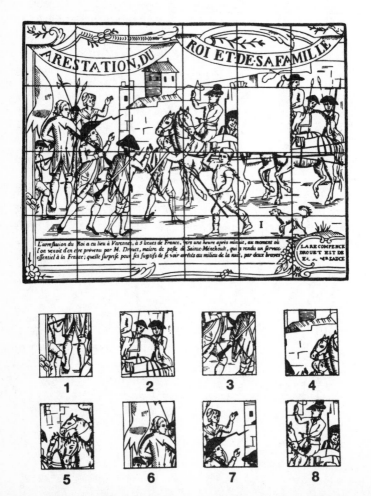

2. Fill in the missing domino.

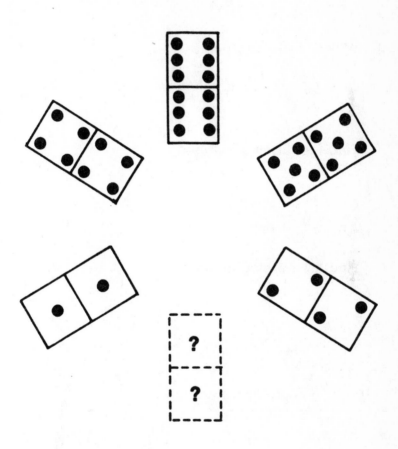

3. Which word completes the following sentence?

'Caffeine is to coffee what nicotine is to . . .'.

tobacco, alcohol, tea, cocoa.

4. Which is the odd one out?

cone, cylinder, cube, sphere, trapezium

5. Find the missing number.

$$39 \ (64) \ 43$$
$$42 \ (\ ? \ ) \ 47$$

6. Find the missing number.

7. How many different maps of France are there?

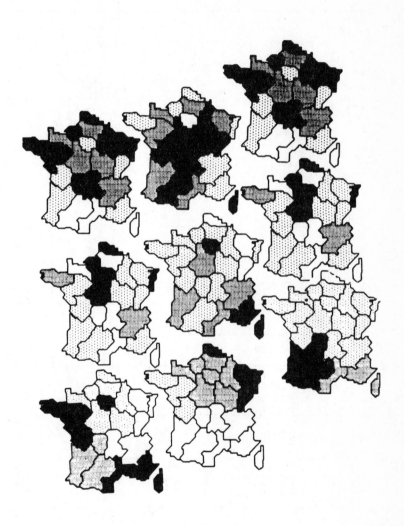

8. Which figure completes the sequence?

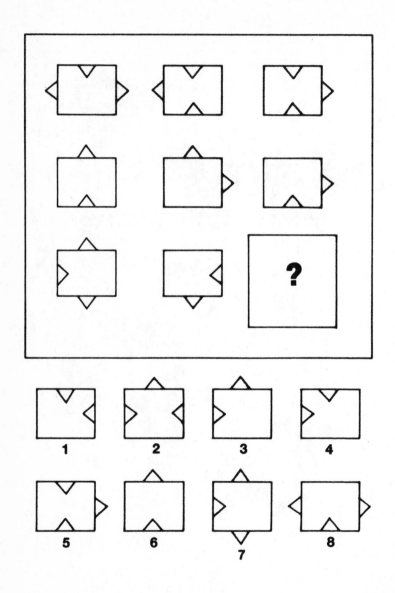

9. **How many blocks are needed for this structure to form a parallelipede?**

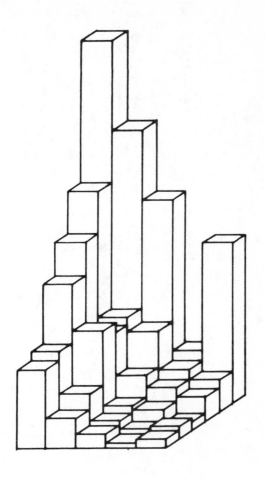

10. What are the hidden cards?

11. **Find a word which forms a differnt word with each of the preceding letters.**

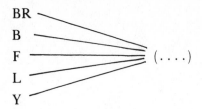

12. **Which is the odd word out?**

TRAPOR
OKUOCC
BLODEU
GUNPINE

13. **Which word goes in the brackets?**

RUBBISH (REFUSE) PREVENT
AIR (. . . .) REEL

14. **Find the missing number.**

10	6	5	12
8	8	16	4
13	9	?	3

15. **Find the missing number.**

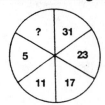

16. Find the missing numbers.

2	7	17	29	?
43	47	53	59	?

17. Study this chessboard closely for 30 seconds. Take a mental note of the position of each piece. Then cover the board . . .

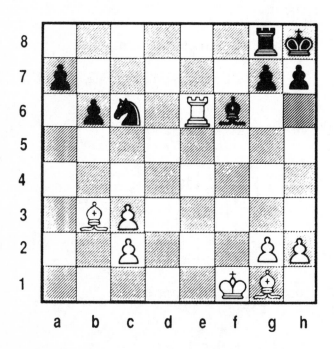

Try and remember the position of the black Knight.

18. Which figure completes the sequence?

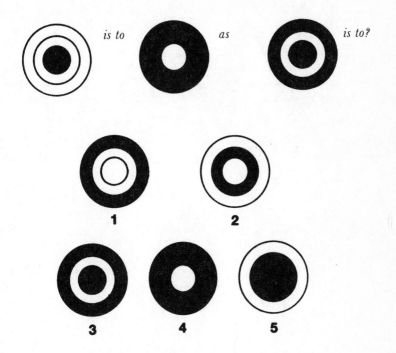

19. Look at these two shapes. The same pyramid is
    shown twice; once in three dimensions and once
    flat. Mark the shaded areas on the flat pyramid.

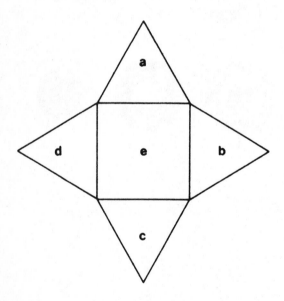

20. Which figure completes the sequence?

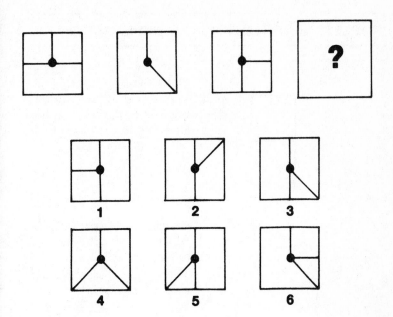

Day Five: solutions

PROBLEM No.	SOLUTION	EXPLANATION
1	5	Piece number five completes the picture.
2	Double zero	The sum of the two dominoes opposite each other always adds up to six in each half of the dominoes.
3	tobacco	Caffeine is the stimulant in coffee, just as nicotine is in tobacco.
4	trapezium	The only quadrilateral amongst solids.
5	125	The number in brackets is obtained by subtracting the left hand number from the right hand number and cubing the result: $43 - 39 = 4\,(^3) = 64$ $47 - 42 = 5\,(^3) = 125$
6	2	In each triangle, the top number is obtained by subtracting one base number from the other: $24 - 17 = 7 \qquad 21 - 19 = 2$
7	7	There are seven different maps of France amongst the nine shown.
8	2	On each line, the right hand figure is obtained by superimposing the two preceding it. Identical exterior triangles cancel each other out.

PROBLEM No.	SOLUTION	EXPLANATION
9	29	29 is the minimum number of additional blocks needed to form a parallelipede from this structure.
10	Seven of Hearts Eight of Clubs	The figure shows a sequence of five Spades and five Clubs alternating between interior and exterior in a clockwise direction. From the five of Spades the cards increase by one each time, just as they do from the four of Clubs.
11	east	Which forms the words: breast, beast, feast, least and yeast.
12	BLODEU = DOUBLE	The rest are anagrams of birds: parrot, cuckoo, penguin.
13	wind	With a different pronunciation 'refuse' means the same as 'rubbish' and 'prevent'. With a different pronunciation 'wind' means the same as 'air' and 'reel'.
14	39	On each horizontal line, the third number is obtained by multiplying the two preceding numbers, and dividing the result by the fourth number: $10 \times 6 = 60/12 = 5$ $8 \times 8 = 64/4 = 16$ $13 \times 9 = 117/3 = 39$

PROBLEM No. SOLUTION EXPLANATION

15	2	Working anti-clockwise, the sequence is that of prime numbers, with one prime number being omitted each time: 31 (29) 23 (19) 17 (13) 11 (7) 5 (3) 2.

16

The top squares follow a sequence of prime numbers, with 2 prime numbers being omitted each time:
2 (3, 5) 7 (11, 13) 17 (19, 23) 29 (31, 37) 41.

In the bottom squares, the sequence of prime numbers is continued, with none being omitted:
43, 47, 53, 59 and 61.

17

The black Knight's position is C6, which you should have found by memorising the coordinates.

18   2

In each pair of figures, the white areas become black and vice-versa.

20   5

The vertical line remains stationary. The left hand line turns 90° clockwise each time, and the right hand line turns 45° clockwise.

	Day one	Day two	Day three	Day four	Day five
Perception	Number of questions: 10 Correct answers: No answers:				Number of questions: 5 (1, 7, 9, 17, 19) Correct answers: No answers:
Language		Number of questions: 10 Correct answers: No answers:			Number of questions: 5 (3, 4, 11, 12, 13) Correct answers: No answers:
Logic			Number of questions: 10 Correct answers: No answers:		Number of questions: 5 (2, 8, 10, 18, 20) Correct answers: No answers:
Numeracy				Number of questions: 10 Correct answers: No answers:	Number of questions: 5 (5, 6, 14, 15, 16) Correct answers: No answers:
	TOTAL QUESTIONS: 40 TOTAL CORRECT ANSWERS:				TOTAL QUESTIONS: 20 TOTAL ANSWERS: ...

Your performance

Each correct answer is worth one point, regardless of difficulty.

Fill in your scores on the table opposite to give you a detailed impression of how you did.

Take note of the number of 'no answers'. This gives you a good indication of any strengths or weaknesses you may have in a particular subject.

By following this programme you can judge your progress:
— in each subject,
— in all four subjects as a whole.

• Subject by subject:

Compare this performance with your previous ones (see the preceding chapter 'Assess yourself'.

• All four subjects as a whole:

Work out your I.Q. from the series of tests you have just done, and compare it with your previous I.Q. score. Take the number of correct answers from the past four days. Divide this by two and add to it the number of correct answers you obtained on day five. This will give you a number between 0 and 40. Mark this on the I.Q. curve in the previous chapter, and follow the instructions given.

Don't worry if you haven't made any noticeable improvement, or even if your score has got worse, because the last series of tests were notably more difficult than the previous ones.

LONG PROGRAMME
WEEKEND ONE

The long programme is normally completed over four weekends. Realistically you need just over half an hour for each section.

If you want to follow a more intense training period, you can if you wish, complete it in four days, with the first day acting as a short programme.

The weekend programme is made up of 40 exercises, with 10 in each of the following 'subjects': perception, language, logic, numbers.

You can work out your progress at the end of each weekend by:

— comparing your results in each subject with your previous results.

— working out a new I.Q. score for all the subjects as a whole.

ATTENTION: YOU HAVE 30 MINUTES TO SOLVE 40 PROBLEMS, WHILE REMEMBERING THE INSTRUCTIONS AND FOLLOWING THE ADVICE GIVEN IN PREVIOUS CHAPTERS.

Perception: problems

1. All these numbers are identical (apart from size) except one. Which one?

2. **Which of the three shapes shown below completes this map of Belgium and Luxembourg?**

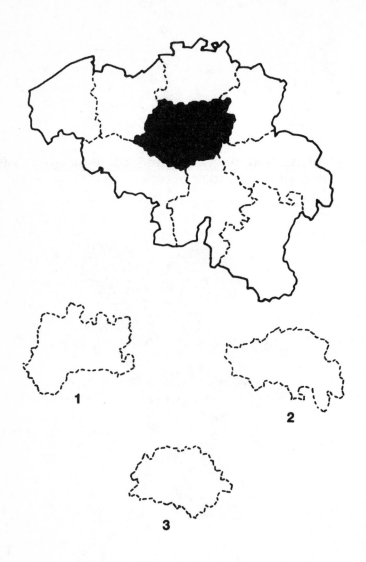

3. How many different patterns are present?

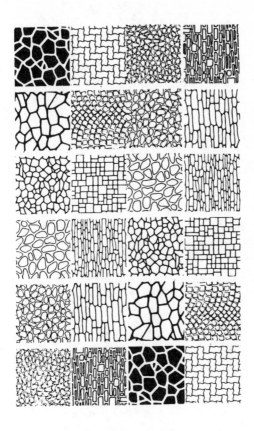

4. Spot the difference between these two pictures.

5. Look at this shape. With which other shape (a, b or c) does it fit together?

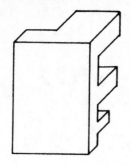

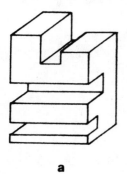

a

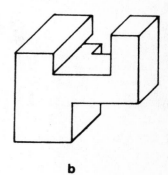

b

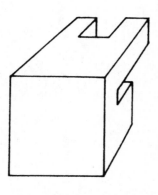

c

6. Each of these Arabic letters is shown twice except one. Which one?

7. **Study this chessboard carefully for 30 seconds. Make a mental note of the position of each playing piece. Cover the board . . .**

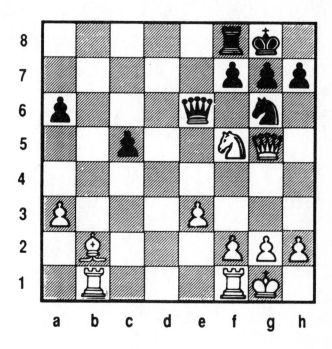

Then find the position of the white Knight from memory.

8. How many left hands and right hands are there?

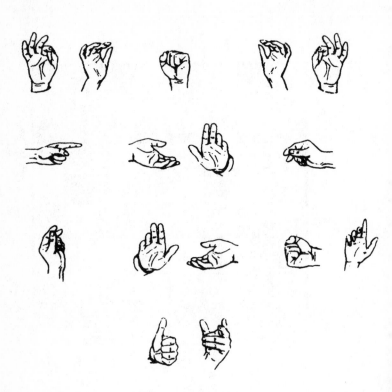

9. How many sides does this solid have?

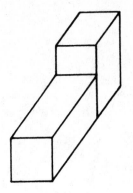

10. Spot the difference between these two nearly identical pictures.

Language: problems

1. **Find a word which forms two different words with the letters outside the brackets.**

   LA (. . . .) ATE   (*Synonym:* examine)

2. **WHich is the odd word out?**

   RULNUMAB
   CEPURS
   PRUTIN
   SNETTUCH

3. **Fill in the brackets.**

   TIMEOUS (STEAM) MARITIME
   GARMENT (. . . . .) NOUMENON

4. **Fill in the brackets with a word that forms a different word with each preceding letter(s).**

   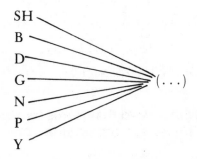

5. **Which word completes the following sentence?**

   'Grain is to a mill what bread is to . . .'.

   a plane, a tree, an oven, a basket.

6. Which is the odd one out?

turbot, john dory, dab, sole, whiting, skate

7. Fill in the brackets with a word that forms a different word with each preceding letter(s).

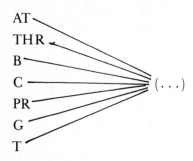

AT
THR
B
C
PR
G
T

(. . .)

8. Fill in the brackets.

REKINDLE (SPINE) PRESSURE
ASTONISH (. . . . .) REEDPIPE

9. Fill in the brackets.

DOORWAY (ENTRANCE) DELIGHT
TINY (. . . . . .) MEMORANDUM

10. Fill in the brackets with a word that forms two different words with the letters either side.

DO (. . . .) STAY

Logic: problems

1. Which figure completes the sequence?

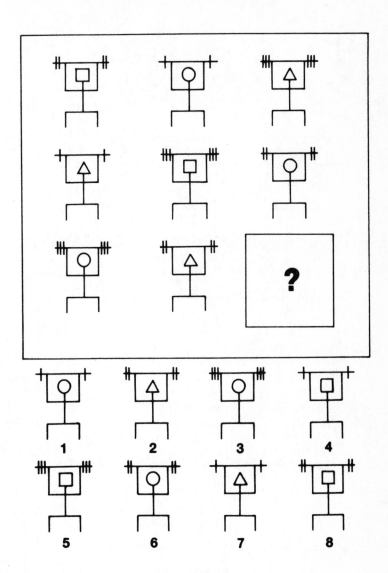

2. Which figure, of the six shown below, completes the sequence?

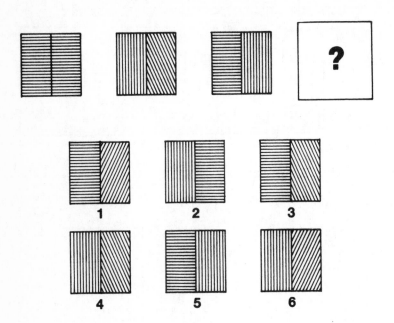

3. What is the hidden card?

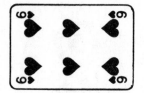

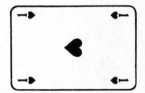

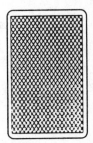

4. Which figure completes the sequence?

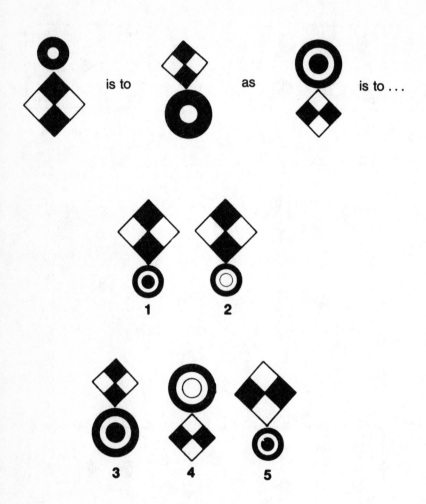

is to

as

is to . . .

1   2

3   4   5

5. Fill in the missing domino.

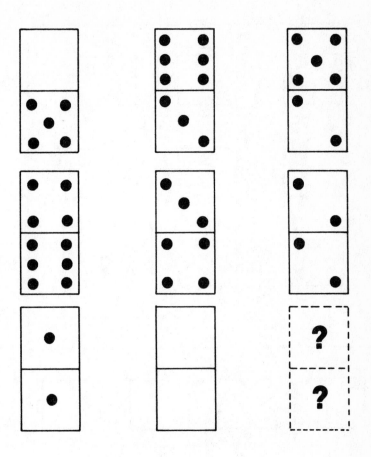

6. Which figure completes the sequence?

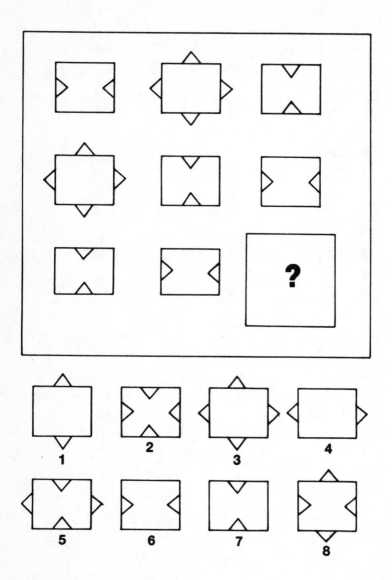

7. Which figure completes the sequence?

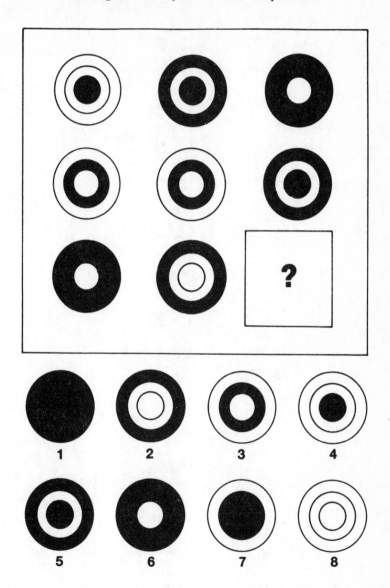

8. Fill in the missing domino.

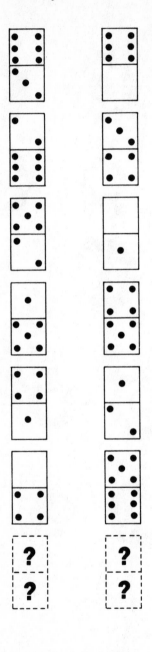

9. Which figure completes the sequence?

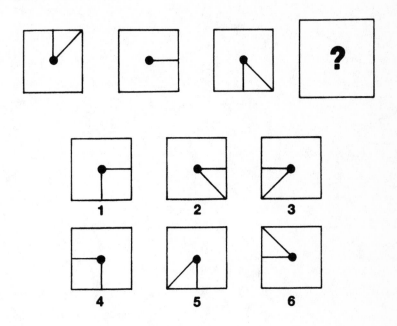

10. What is the missing card?

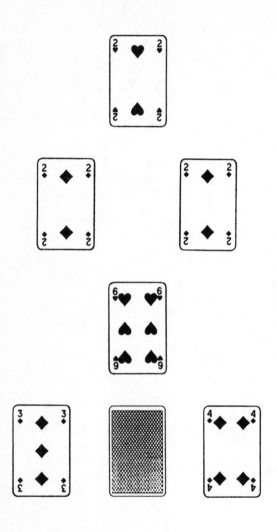

Numbers: problems

1. Find the missing number.

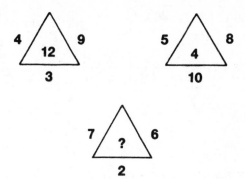

2. Find the missing number.

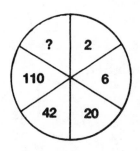

3. Find the missing number.

63 (21) 9
48 (?) 6

4. Find the missing number.

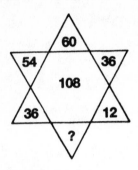

5. Find the missing numbers.

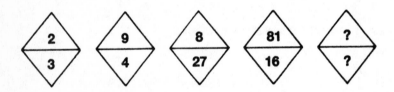

6. Find the missing number.

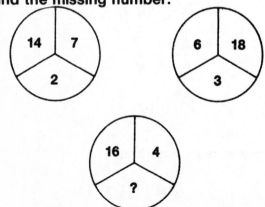

7. Find the missing number.

8. Find the missing numbers.

4	4	10	8	22	12	?
2	6	6	14	10	26	?

9. Find the missing number.

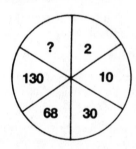

10. Find the missing number.

7	5	4	8
9	3	3	18
?	7	5	15

Solutions

Perception

PROBLEM No.	SOLUTION
1	The second number to the right of biggest 'two' is slightly different from the others; the top of the number is slightly more closed.
2	Piece number three completes the map.
3	The patchwork is made up of 12 different patterns.
4	A small star is missing on the lion's hind leg in the second picture.
5	The shape fits together with figure 'a'.
6	The first letter of the group of three at the bottom on the right is the only letter not to be shown twice.
7	The white Knight's position is F5, to be remembered by its coordinates.
8	There are nine left hands and seven right hands.
9	The shape has eight sides.
10	A claw is missing on the lion's paw at the top right of the second picture.

PROBLEM No.	SOLUTION	EXPLANATION
1	test	Which forms the words: latest and testate.
2	PRUTIN = TURNIP	The rest are anagrams of trees: laburnum, spruce, chestnut.
3	tenor	The first and last letters of the word in brackets are the last and third letters of the word to the left of it. The second, third and fourth letters are the fifth, last and second letters of the word to the right of it.
4	ear	Which forms the words: shear, bear, dear, gear, near, pear and year.
5	oven	An oven is used for bread just as a mill is used for grain.
6	whiting	A whiting is the only one that is not a flat fish.
7	one	Which forms the words: atone, throne, bone, cone, prone, gone and tone.
8	prone	The first, second and fifth letters of the word in brackets are the fifth, first and last letters of the right hand word. The third and fourth are the fourth and fifth letters of the left hand word.
9	minute	With a different pronunciation 'entrance' means the same as both the

PROBLEM No.	SOLUTION	EXPLANATION
		words outside the brackets. With a different pronunciation 'minute' means the same as both the words outside the brackets.
10	main	Which forms the words: domain and mainstay.

Logic

PROBLEM No.	SOLUTION	EXPLANATION
1	4	On each line, the head is represented alternately by a circle, a square and a rectangle. The dumb-bells have two, four or six discs.
2	6	On the left side, the stripes are alternately horizontal and vertical. On the right, the stripes turn 45° clockwise.
3	Five of Clubs	Each line is made up of one suit: Hearts, Clubs and Diamonds. On each line, when the two cards are added together, the total is always seven: $6 + 1 = 2 + 5 = 4 + 3 = 7$.

PROBLEM No.	SOLUTION	EXPLANATION

4   5

In the second figure of each pair, the diamond and circle swap positions, and their sizes are reversed.

5   6/1

The top half of each domino follows the sequence 0, 6, 5, 4, 3, 2, 1, 0, 6. The bottom half of the right hand domino on each line is obtained by subtracting the bottom half of the second domino from the bottom half of the first.

6   3

The same three figures are present on each line, but in a different order.

7   7

On each line, the right hand figure is obtained by superimposing the two preceding figures, with identical colours changing colour. i.e. black + black = white, white + white = black.

8   3/0   2/3

In the left column the numbers decrease in value, with two numbers being omitted between each domino half. In the right column, the numbers increase in value, with two numbers being omitted between each domino:

PROBLEM No. SOLUTION   EXPLANATION

[6 (5,4) 3] [2 (1,0) 6]
[5 (4,3) 2] [1 (0,6) 5]
[4 (3,2) 1] [0 (6,5) 4]
[3 (2,1) 0].
and: 6/0 (1,2) 3/4 (5,6) 0/1
(2,3) 4/5 (6,0) 1/2 (3,4) 5/6
(0,1) 2/3.

9      4 The vertical line moves 90°
clockwise each time, the
other one moves 45° clockwise each time.

10   Ace of diamonds   The suit on the cards alter-
nates between Hearts and
Diamonds. Working from
the top downwards, the
value, or sum of values on
the cards increases by two
on each line.

2, (2 + 2 =) 4, 6,
(3 + 1 + 4 =) 8

Numbers

PROBLEM No. SOLUTION   EXPLANATION

1   7 /21\ 6   The number in the middle
        2   of each triangle is obtained
by multiplying together the
two side numbers, and dividing the result by the base
number:
$4 \times 9 = 36/3 = 12$
$5 \times 8 = 40/10 = 4$
$7 \times 6 = 42/2 = 21$

2   156   The sequence is a progression of prime numbers.
Each number corresponds

PROBLEM No.	SOLUTION	EXPLANATION

to the difference between a number squared, and itself:
$2^2 - 2 = 2$, $3^2 - 3 = 6$, $5^2 - 5 = 20$, $7^2 - 7 = 42$, $11^2 - 11 = 110$, $13^2 - 13 = 156$.

3   **24**

The number in brackets is obtained by dividing the two numbers outside the brackets and multiplying the result by 3:
$63/9 = 7 \times 3 = 21$
$48/6 = 8 \times 3 = 24$

4   **18**

In both triangles, when all three corner numbers are added together, the result must be 108, the centre number:
$60 + 36 + 12 = 108 = 54 + 36 + (18)$

5

Starting with the two on the left, and alternating between top and bottom, the numbers increase by being multiplied by two each time:
$2 = 2$, $2^2 = 4$, $2^3 = 8$, $2^4 = 16$, $2^5 = 32$.
The other halves increase by being multiplied by three each time:
$3 = 3$, $3^2 = 9$, $3^3 = 27$, $3^4 = 81$, $3^5 = 243$.

6   **4**

In each circle, the bottom number is obtained by dividing the greater of the two side numbers by the smaller one:
$14/7 = 2$, $18/6 = 3$ and $16/4 = 4$.

7   **2210**

The sequence is a progression of prime numbers.

PROBLEM No.	SOLUTION	EXPLANATION

| | | Each number corresponds to a prime number, cubed, and added to itself: $2^3 + 2 = 10$, $3^3 + 3 = 30$, $5^3 + 5 = 130$, $7^3 + 7 = 350$, $11^3 + 11 = 1342$, $13^3 + 13 = 2210$. |

8

34
14

Starting with the four at the top left, and alternating top and bottom, the progression is prime numbers + themselves:
$2 + 2 = 4$, $3 + 3 = 6$,
$5 + 5 = 10$, $7 + 7 = 14$,
$11 + 11 = 22$,
$13 + 13 = 26$,
$17 + 17 = 34$.
The other halves are whole numbers + themselves:
$1 + 1 = 2$, $2 + 2 = 4$,
$3 + 3 = 6$, $4 + 4 = 8$,
$5 + 5 = 10$, $6 + 6 = 12$,
$7 + 7 = 14$.

9   222

The sequence is a progression of whole numbers. Each number is a whole number, cubed, and added to itself:
$1^3 + 1 = 2$, $2^3 + 2 = 10$,
$3^3 + 3 = 30$, $4^3 + 4 = 68$,
$5^3 + 5 = 130$, $6^3 + 6 = 222$.

10   10

On each line, the left hand number is obtained by dividing the fourth number by the third, and adding the second number to the result:
$8/4 = 2 + 5 = 7$
$18/3 = 6 + 3 = 9$
$15/5 = 3 + 7 = 10$.

Your performance

Award yourself one point for each correct answer and write your different scores into the table below.

WEEKEND ONE	
PERCEPTION	Number of questions: 10 Correct answers:
LANGUAGE	Number of questions: 10 Correct answers:
LOGIC	Number of questions: 10 Correct answers:
NUMBERS	Number of questions: 10 Correct answers:
	TOTAL QUESTIONS: 40 TOTAL ANSWERS: ..

Refer to the I.Q. curve on page 104 in the chapter 'Assess Yourself'. Work out your intellect level and the progress you are making.

LONG PROGRAMME
WEEKEND TWO

ATTENTION: YOU HAVE 30 MINUTES TO
SOLVE 40 PROBLEMS, WHILE
REMEMBERING THE INSTRUCTIONS AND
FOLLOWING THE ADVICE GIVEN IN
PREVIOUS CHAPTERS.

Language: problems

1. **Fill in the brackets with a word that forms a different word with each preceding letter(s).**

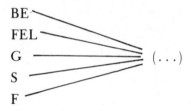

BE
FEL
G
S
F
(...)

2. **What word goes in the brackets?**

> DOWN (CAST) IRON
> HOT (...) SIDE

3. **What word goes in the brackets?**

> LONG (RANGE) FINDER
> SNAP (....) GUN

4. **Find a word which forms two different words with the letters outside the brackets.**

> OX (...) LER

5. **Which word completes the following sentence?**

A pentagon is to five as a heptagon is to . . . . . ?

6. **Which is the odd one out?**

motley, mottled, spangled, speckled, variegated, plain

7. **Find a word which forms two different words when placed with the letters outside the brackets.**

GO (. .) LAS

8. **Which is the odd word out?**

EGMILT
HPCUN
CREWHN
CAFRIB

9. **Fill in the brackets.**

SERIOUS (NURSE) REMNANT
SINGLET (. . . . .) AEOLIAN

10. Fill in the brackets with a word that forms a different word with each preceding letter(s).

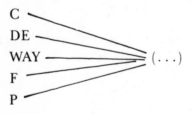

C
DE
WAY (. . .)
F
P

Logic: problems

1. Which figure completes the sequence?

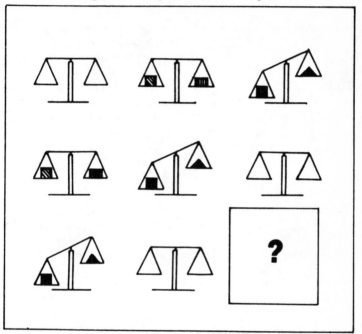

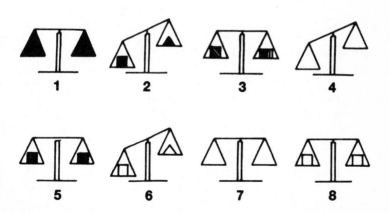

2. Which figure, of the five shown, completes the sequence?

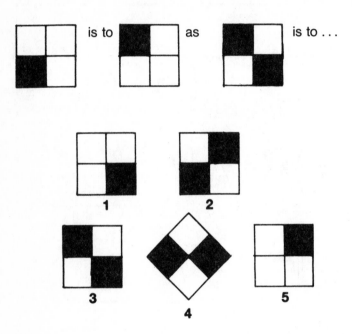

3. Find the hidden card.

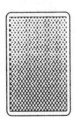

4. Which figure completes the sequence?

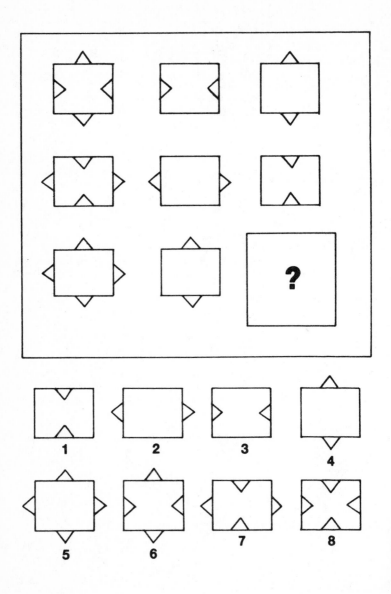

5. Fill in the missing domino.

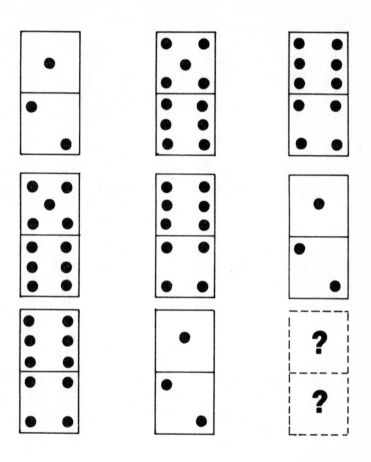

6. Which figure completes the sequence?

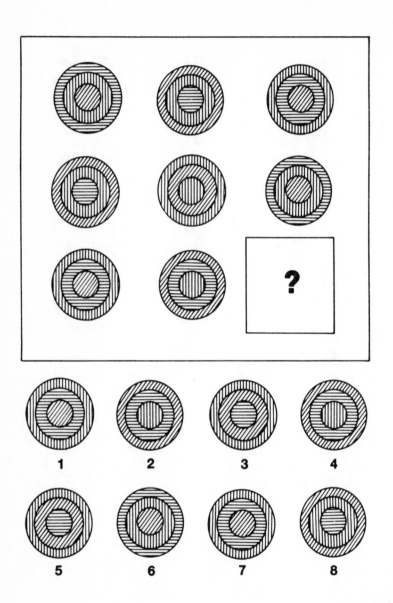

7. Find the hidden cards.

8. **Which figure is the odd one out?**

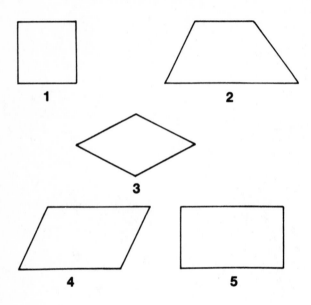

9. **Which figure, of the six below, completes the sequence?**

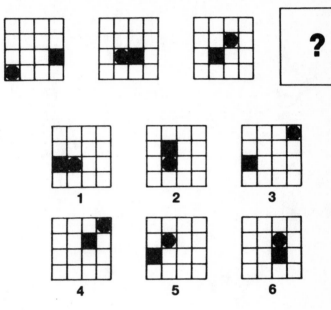

10. Which figure completes the sequence?

Numbers: problems

1. Find the missing number.

9	3	12
8	5	6
7	2	?

2. Find the missing number.

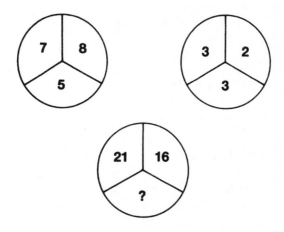

3. Find the missing number.

432 (95) 527
328 (?) 411

4. Find the missing number.

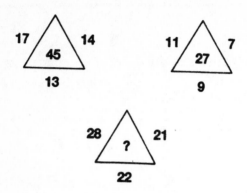

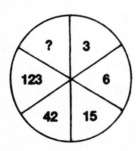

5. Find the missing number.

5	4	6	3
12	3	7	8
7	11	9	?

6. Find the missing number.

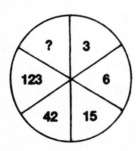

7. Find the missing numbers.

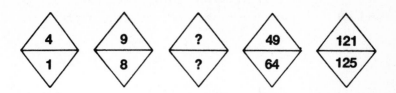

8. Find the missing number.

1	2	5
2	3	13
3	1	?

9. Find the missing number.

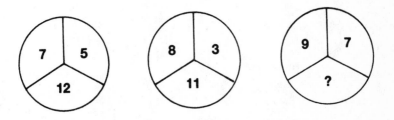

10. Find the missing numbers.

1	3	5	7	?
1	9	25	49	?

Perception: problems

1. How many different E's are there?

2. **This shape has been made by folding one of the three figures below (a, b, c). Which one?**

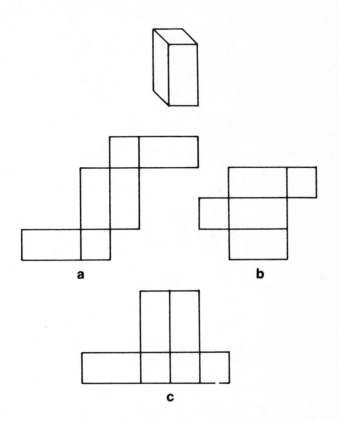

3. Spot the difference between these two pictures.

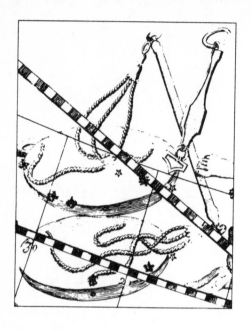

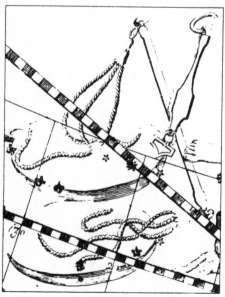

4. When this shape is rotated 45° to the right, which figure does it become? (1, 2, 3)

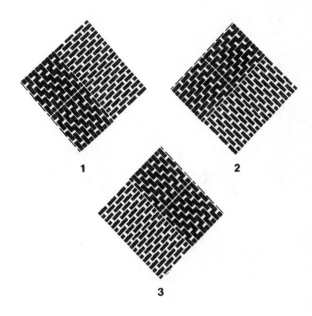

5. How many different faces are present in this picture?

6. **Look at these shapes. How many different sizes are present?**

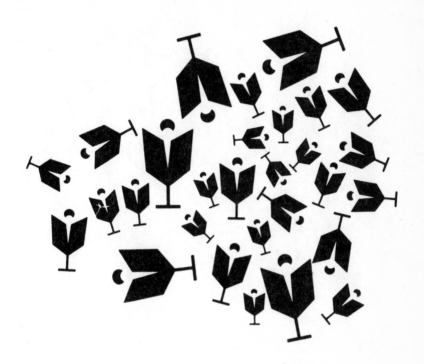

7. Which figure (1, 2, 3) completes this map of Switzerland?

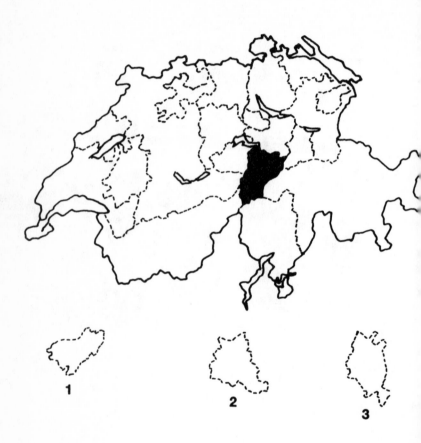

1

2

3

8. How many sides does this solid have?

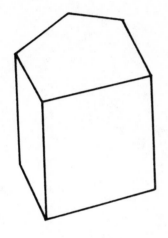

9. Spot the difference between these two pictures.

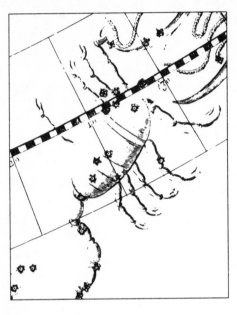

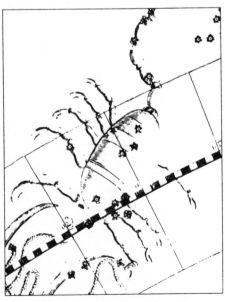

10. **Study this chessboard for 30 seconds. Make a mental note of the position of each piece. Then cover the board ...**

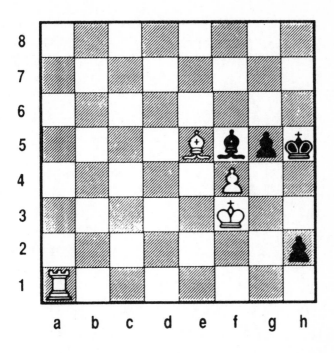

Find the position of the white King from memory.

Solutions

Language

PROBLEM No.	SOLUTION	EXPLANATION
1	low	Which forms the words: below, fellow, glow, slow and flow.
2	bed	It can go after 'hot' and before 'side'.
3	shot	It can go after 'snap' and before 'gun'.
4	bow	Which forms the words: oxbow and bowler.
5	seven	The number of sides in the figure.
6	plain	All the other adjectives suggest multicolour.
7	at	Which forms the words: goat and atlas.
8	CAFRIB = FABRIC	The rest are anagrams of tools: gimlet, punch, wrench.
9	lease	The first, third and fifth letters of the word in brackets are the fourth, first and second leters of the right hand word. The second and fourth letters are the sixth and first letters of the left hand word.

PROBLEM No.	SOLUTION	EXPLANATION
10	lay	Which forms the words: clay, delay, waylay, flay and play.

Logic

PROBLEM No.	SOLUTION	EXPLANATION

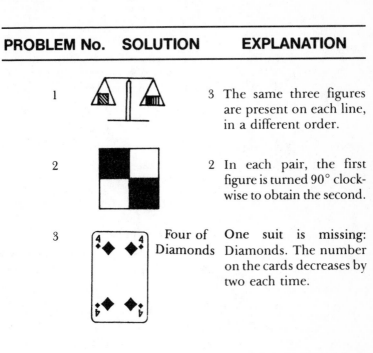

1   3 The same three figures are present on each line, in a different order.

2   2 In each pair, the first figure is turned 90° clockwise to obtain the second.

3   Four of Diamonds   One suit is missing: Diamonds. The number on the cards decreases by two each time.

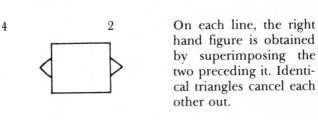

4   2 On each line, the right hand figure is obtained by superimposing the two preceding it. Identical triangles cancel each other out.

PROBLEM No.	SOLUTION	EXPLANATION

5   5/6

The same three dominoes are present on each line, in a different order.

6   6

The same three patterns are present in the exterior rings on each line, in a different order.

7   Four of Hearts   Six of Diamonds

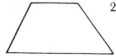

Starting with the Ace of Hearts and alternating interior/exterior, the progression is whole numbers of the same suit: Hearts, 1, 2, 3, 4, 5. The same is true with the Diamonds, but the numbers increase by two each time: 2, 4, 6, 8, 10.

8

2   Number 2, the trapezium is the odd one out because it is the only shape with just two parallel sides.

9   3

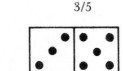

The circle moves one place diagonally from bottom to top each time. The square moves one place horizontally from right to left each time.

10   3/5

Starting with the 3 on the domino 3/6, the progression is:
4 is the 1st number after 3
6 is the 2nd number after 4
2 is the 3rd number after 6
6 is the 4th number after 2
4 is the 5th number after 6
3 is the 6th number after 4
On the other halves, the progression is whole numbers: 6, 0, 1, 2, 3, 4, 5.

Numbers

PROBLEM No.	SOLUTION	EXPLANATION
1	10	The right hand number is obtained by subtracting the second number from the first and doubling the result: $9 - 3 = 6 \times 2 = 12$ $8 - 5 = 3 \times 2 = 6$ $7 - 2 = 5 \times 2 = 10$
2	15	In the third circle each number is equal to the two corresponding numbers in the preceding two circles when multiplied together: $7 \times 3 = 21, 8 \times 2 = 16,$ $5 \times 3 = 15.$
3	83	The number in brackets is obtained by subtracting the left hand number from the right hand number: $527 - 432 = 95$ $411 - 328 = 83$
4	72	The number in the third triangle is always equal to the two corresponding numbers in the first two triangles when added together: $17 + 11 = 28$ $14 + 7 = 21$ $13 + 9 = 22$ and $45 + 27 = 72$.
5	9	On each line, the fourth number is obtained by adding together the first two numbers, and subtracting the third number from the result: $5 + 4 = 9 - 6 = 3$ $12 + 3 = 15 - 7 = 8$ $7 + 11 = 18 - 9 = 9$

PROBLEM No.	SOLUTION	EXPLANATION

6   366

The progression follows the pattern $(\times 3 - 3)$:
$3 (\times 3 = 9 - 3 =) 6 (\times 3 = 18 - 3 =) 15 (\times 3 = 45 - 3 =) 42 (\times 3 = 126 - 3 =) 123 (\times 3 = 369 - 3 =) 366$.

7

In the top triangle, the progression is that of prime numbers, squared. In the bottom triangle, the progression is that of whole numbers cubed:
$2^2 = 4, 3^2 = 9, 5^2 = 25,$
$7^2 = 49, 11^2 = 121.$
and:
$1^3 = 1, 2^3 = 8, 3^3 = 27,$
$4^3 = 64, 5^3 = 125.$

8   10

On each line, the right hand number is obtained by adding together the two preceding numbers, both squared:
$1^2 + 2^2 = 1 + 4 = 5$
$2^2 + 3^2 = 4 + 9 = 13$
$3^2 + 1^2 = 9 + 1 = 10$

9   16

In each circle, the bottom number is obtained by adding together the two side numbers:
$7 + 5 = 12, 8 + 3 = 11$
and $9 + 7 = 16$.

10

The top square is a progression of odd numbers. The bottom square is these same numbers, squared.

Perception

PROBLEM No.	SOLUTION
1	There are nine different E's in the picture.
2	When unfolded, the shape becomes figure 'a'.
3	The end of the rope is missing in the second picture at the bottom left.
4	When the shape is turned 45° clockwise, it becomes figure two.
5	Of the 15 faces shown, seven are different.
6	The shape is shown 29 times, in five different sizes.
7	Figure 1 completes the map of Switzerland.
8	The solid, a prism, has seven sides.
9	The '1' written on the scorpion's shell is missing in the second picture.
10	The position should be found by remembering the coordinates F3.

Your performance

Award yourself one point for each correct answer and write your different scores into the table below.

WEEKEND TWO	
PERCEPTION	Number of questions: 10 Correct answers:
LANGUAGE	Number of questions: 10 Correct answers:
LOGIC	Number of questions: 10 Correct answers:
NUMBERS	Number of questions: 10 Correct answers:
	TOTAL QUESTIONS: 40 TOTAL ANSWERS: ..

Refer to the I.Q. curve on page 104 in the chapter 'Assess Yourself'. Work out your intellect level and the progress you are making.

LONG PROGRAMME
WEEKEND THREE

ATTENTION: YOU HAVE 30 MINUTES TO
SOLVE 40 PROBLEMS, WHILE
REMEMBERING THE INSTRUCTIONS AND
FOLLOWING THE ADVICE GIVEN IN
PREVIOUS CHAPTERS.

Logic: problems

1. Which figure completes the sequence?

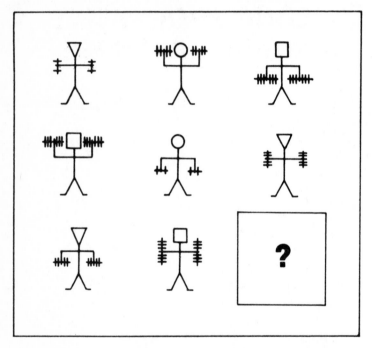

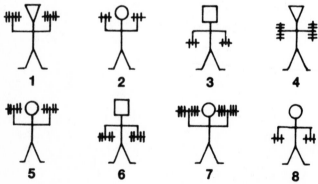

2. Fill in the missing dominoes.

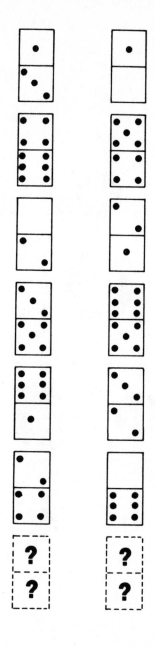

3. Which figure completes the sequence?

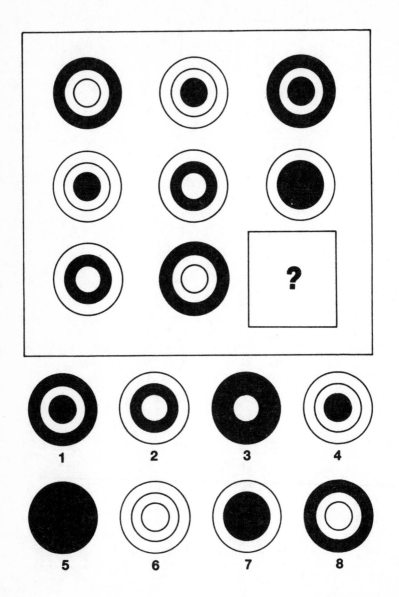

4. Find the hidden card.

5. Which figure completes the sequence?

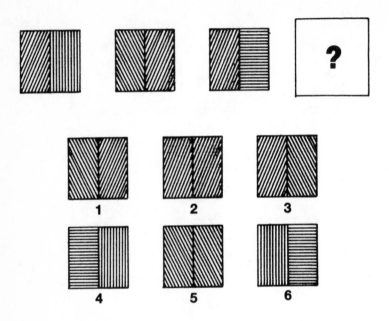

6. Which figure completes the sequence?

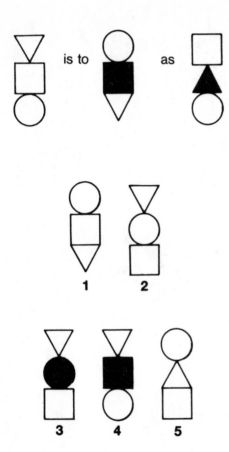

7. Fill in the missing domino.

8. Which figure is the odd one out?

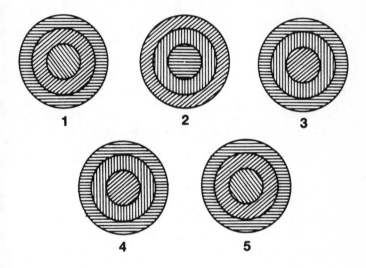

9. Which figure completes the sequence?

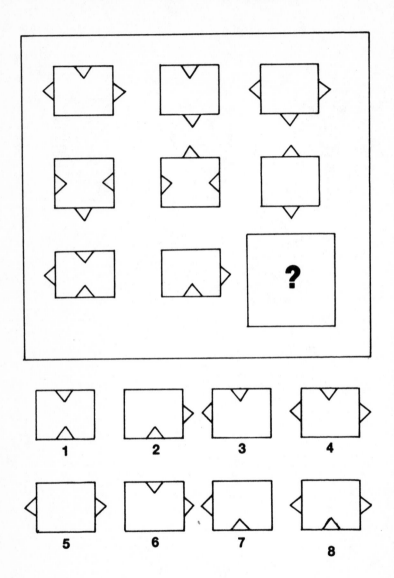

10. What are the hidden cards?

Numbers: problems

1. **Find the missing number.**

7	3	5
8	24	7
9	6	?

2. **Find the missing number.**

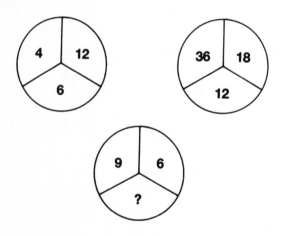

3. **Find the missing number.**

14 (154) 11
13 (?) 9

4. Find the missing number.

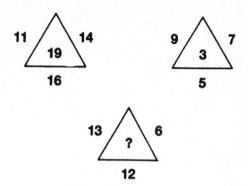

5. Find the missing number.

6	3	5	10
8	2	3	12
4	4	7	?

6. Find the missing number.

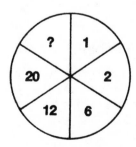

7. Find the missing numbers.

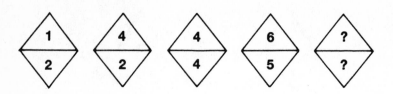

8. Find the missing number.

3	6	9
2	2	4
1	?	1

9. Find the missing number.

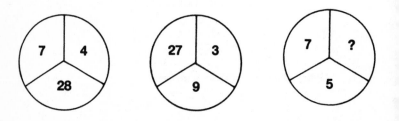

10. Find the missing numbers.

1	8	9	64	?
1	4	27	16	?

Perception: problems

1. How many different objects are present, regardless of size?

2. This shape has been made by folding one of these three figures (a, b, c). Which one?

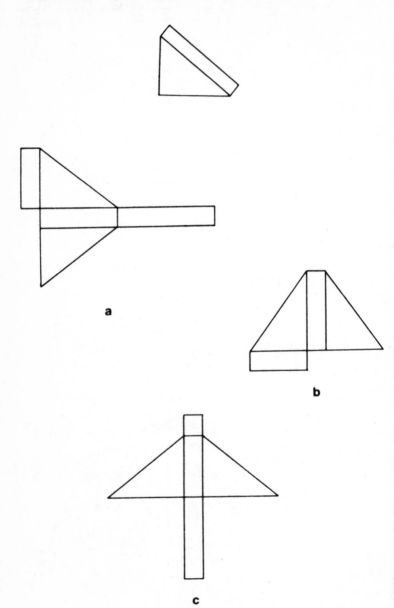

3. Spot the difference between these two pictures.

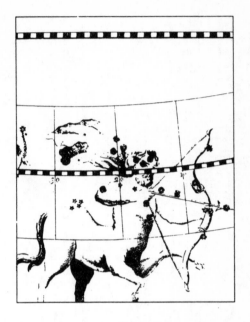

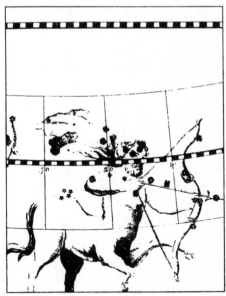

4. **How many different patterns are present in this picture?**

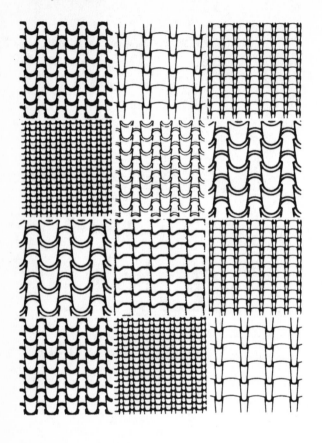

5. How many different symbols are present, regardless of size and position?

6. **Which of the three figures below (1, 2 or 3) matches the part of Italy that has been shaded black on the map?**

7. How many different sports are present in this picture?

8. How many faces does this solid have?

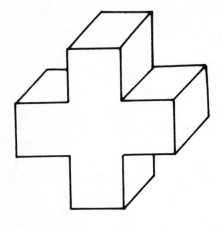

9. Spot the difference between these two pictures.

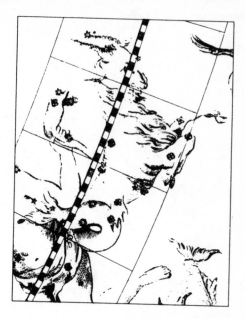

10. **Study this chessboard for 30 seconds. Try and memorise the position of each playing piece. Then cover the board . . .**

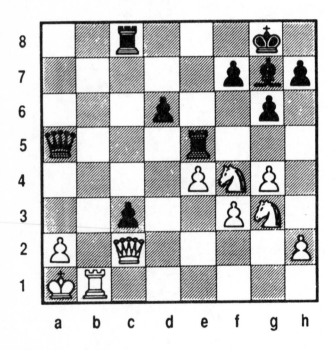

and find the black Queen's position from memory.

Language: problems

1. Fill in the brackets with a word that forms two different words with the letters either side.

   GR (. . .) TONE   *Clue: top card*

2. Which is the odd one out?

   LOIN
   GRITE
   RABE
   TREPHAN

3. What word goes in the brackets?

   CLASS (FORM) BENCH
   FURNACE (. . . . .) IMITATE

4. Fill in the brackets with a word that forms a different word with each preceding letter(s).

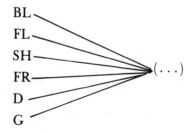

5. Beige is to brown as cerulean is to:

   red, green, grey, blue, black.

6. Which is the odd one out?

   orange, mandarin, lemon, grapefruit, apricot, tomato.

7. **Fill in the brackets with a word that forms a different word with each preceding letter(s).**

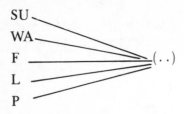

SU
WA
F
L
P
(..)

8. **What word goes in the brackets?**

BUSINESS (FIRM) SOLID
EQUILIBRIUM (......) HORSE BOX

9. **Complete the second line.**

DROP (PRODUCER) CURE
BATS (........) CART

10. **Find a word that forms two different words with the letters outside the brackets.**

MAL (....) ATION

Solutions

Logic

PROBLEM No.	SOLUTION	EXPLANATION
1	2	On each line, the head is represented either by a circle, a triangle or a square. The arms are alternatively horizontal, up or down. The dumb-bells have 4, 8 or 12 discs.
2	5/0 4/3	On the left hand column the numbers progress with one number omitted between each domino half: [1(2)3] [4(5)6] [0(1)2] [3(4)5] [6(0)1] [2(3)4] [5(6)0]. On the right hand column, the numbers decrease, with one number omitted between each whole domino: 1/0 (6) 5/4 (3) 2/1 (0) 6/5 (4) 3/2 (1) 0/6 (5) 4/3.
3	3	On each line, the right hand figure is obtained by superimposing the two preceding ones on one another.
4	Three of Hearts	The same three suits are present on each line in a different order. The Heart is missing on the third line. The value on

PROBLEM No.   SOLUTION   EXPLANATION

the card is obtained by subtracting the middle card from the left hand card:

$9 - 6 = 3$
$6 - 5 = 1$
and $10 - 7 = 3$.

5   5

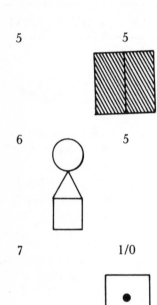

The stripes on the left hand side of the square turn 90° clockwise each time. On the other side, the stripes turn 45° clockwise each time.

6   5

In the second figure of each pair, the middle shape remains in its position but changes colour. The top and bottom shapes change position but stay the same colour.

7   1/0

One half of the dominoes decreases in value by one each time (0, 6, 5, 4, 3, 2, 1). The other half, starting with the 0, progresses as follows: 6 is the first number before 0, 4 is the second number before 6, 1 is the third number before 4, 4 is the fourth number before 1, 6 is the fifth number before 4 and 0 is the sixth number before 6.

8   2

Number 2 is the odd one out because numbers 1 and 5, and 3 and 4 are identical pairs.

PROBLEM No.	SOLUTION	EXPLANATION

| 9 | 4 | On each line the right hand figure is obtained by superimposing the two preceding figures. Identical interior triangles cancel each other out. |

| 10 | Two of Hearts | Each line is made up of the same suit. On the first line the number on the right hand card is found by subtracting the middle card from the left hand card. |

Nine of Spades

On the second line, these two cards are added together to get the right hand card. The third line works like the first, and the fourth line works like the second line.

Numbers

PROBLEM No.	SOLUTION	EXPLANATION

| 1 | 3 | The number in the middle is equal to the sum of all four corner squares added together. It is also equal to the remaining four squares added together: $3 + 6 + 8 + 7 = 24 = 7 + 5 + 9 + (3)$. |

| 2 | 18 | The numbers in the second circle correspond |

PROBLEM No.	SOLUTION	EXPLANATION
		to the numbers in the first circle, tripled. The numbers in the third circle correspond to the numbers in the second circle halved.
3	117	The number in brackets is obtained by multiplying together the two numbers on either side: $14 \times 11 = 154$ $13 \times 9 = 117$
4	5	The numbers in the third triangle are obtained by subtracting the numbers in the second triangle from those in the first. The positions have been changed: $16 - 3 = 13, 11 - 5 = 6,$ $19 - 7 = 12 \,\&\, 14 - 9 = 5.$
5	7	On each line the right hand number is obtained by dividing together the first two numbers and multiplying the result by the third number: $6/3 = 2 \times 5 = 10$ $8/2 = 4 \times 3 = 12$ $4/4 = 1 \times 7 = 7.$
6	30	From the 1 onwards, the progression is that of whole numbers, squared, plus themselves: $1^2 + 1 = 2$ $2^2 + 2 = 6$ $3^2 + 3 = 12$ $4^2 + 4 = 20$ $5^2 + 5 = 30$

—

PROBLEM No.	SOLUTION	EXPLANATION

7

Starting with the 1 in the top left hand triangle, and alternating top and bottom, the progression follows the sequence +1, ×2:
1 (+1=) 2 (×2=)
4 (+1=) 5 (×2=) 10.
Following the same system, the other halves follow the sequence +2, ×1:
2 (+2=) 4 (×1=) 4(+2=)
6 (×1=) 6.

8   0

The middle square on each line is obtained by subtracting the left hand number from the right hand number:
$9 - 3 = 6$
$4 - 2 = 2$
$1 - 1 = 0$

9   35

In each circle, the biggest number is obtained by multiplying together the other two numbers:
$7 \times 4 = 28$
$9 \times 3 = 27$
$7 \times 5 = 35$

10

25
125

Starting with the 1 in the top left hand square, and alternating top and bottom, the sequence is that of whole numbers, squared. Following the same system in the other squares, the sequence is that of whole numbers, cubed:
$1^2 = 1, 2^2 = 4, 3^2 = 9, 4^2 = 16, 5^2 = 25$.
and $1^3 = 1, 2^3 = 8, 3^3 = 27, 4^3 = 64, 5^3 = 125$.

Perception

PROBLEM No.	SOLUTION
1	Six different objects are present: a telephone, a television, a typewriter, a bin, a timer, a box.
2	When unfolded, the shape becomes figure 'a'.
3	A tiny star is missing at the top left of the second picture near the Capricorn's ear.
4	Seven different patterns are present in the picture.
5	Five different symbols are present.
6	Figure 1 completes the map of Italy.
7	Eleven different sports are represented in this picture.
8	This solid has 14 sides.
9	A stripe is missing on the central line of the second picture, four from the bottom.
10	The position a5 should be found by memorising the coordinates.

Language

PROBLEM No.	SOLUTION	EXPLANATION
1	ace	Which forms the words: grace and acetone.
2	RABE	When the anagrams are solved, BEAR is the only one that is not part of the cat family. (LION, TIGER, PANTHER).

PROBLEM No.	SOLUTION	EXPLANATION
3	forge	A synonym of furnace and imitate, as form is of class and bench.
4	own	Which forms the words: blown, flown, shown, frown, down and gown.
5	blue	Beige is a shade of brown, cerulean is a shade of blue.
6	apricot	The only fruit with a stone; all the others have pips.
7	it	Which forms the words: suit, wait, fit, lit and pit.
8	stable	A synonym of equilibrium and horse box, as firm is of business and solid.
9	abstract	Bats is an anagram of the first four letters of abstract and cart is an anagram of the second four.
10	form	Which forms the words: malform and formation.

Your performance

Award yourself one point for each correct answer and write your different scores into the table below.

WEEKEND THREE	
PERCEPTION	Number of questions: 10 Correct answers:
LANGUAGE	Number of questions: 10 Correct answers:
LOGIC	Number of questions: 10 Correct answers:
NUMBERS	Number of questions: 10 Correct answers:
	TOTAL QUESTIONS: 40 TOTAL ANSWERS: . .

Refer to the I.Q. curve on page 104 in the chapter 'Assess Yourself'. Work out your intellect level and the progress you are making.

LONG PROGRAMME
WEEKEND FOUR

ATTENTION: YOU HAVE 30 MINUTES TO SOLVE 40 PROBLEMS, WHILE REMEMBERING THE INSTRUCTIONS AND FOLLOWING THE ADVICE GIVEN IN PREVIOUS CHAPTERS.

Numbers: problems

1. Find the missing numbers.

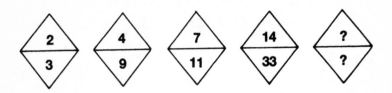

2. Find the missing numbers.

2	6	10
3	24	30
4	?	?

3. Find the missing number.

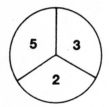 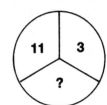 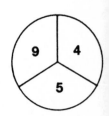

4. Find the missing numbers.

2
4

16
4

6
36

64
8

?
?

5. Find the missing number.

8	3	4	6
5	4	10	2
9	2	6	?

6. Find the missing number.

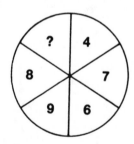

7. Find the missing number.

21 (116) 37
27 (?) 73

8. Find the missing number.

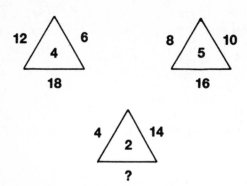

9. Find the missing number.

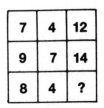

7	4	12
9	7	14
8	4	?

10. Find the missing number.

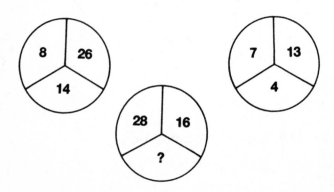

Language: problems

1. **Fill in the brackets with a word that forms a different word with each of the preceding letters.**

NO
SER
AD
DE
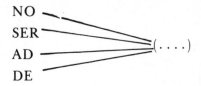
(. . . .)

2. **Which word goes in the brackets?**

TEAR (RETAINER) REIN
ROME (. . . . .) ROVE

3. **Fill in the brackets on the second line.**

NUMERACY (ENTER) MEANTIME
REPORTER (. . . . .) EMIGRATE

4. **Find a word which, when placed in the brackets, forms two different words with the letters either side.**

TI (. . .) GO

5. **What word completes the following phrase?**

The bullet is to a gun what the bolt is to . . .

an arquebus, a crossbow, a bow, a spear

6. **Which is the odd word out?**

fascinate, allure, charm, enrich, intrigue.

7. Find a word which forms two different words with the letters either side. *Clue: boy.*

PAR (. . .) NET

8. Which is the odd one out?

ELOS
NOSLAM
GRITE
TAUN

9. What word goes in the brackets?

DESIRE (WANT) POVERTY
SEQUEL (. . . .) FUNERAL

10. Fill in the brackets with a word that forms a different word with each preceding letter.

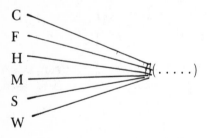

Perception: problems

1. Which figure (1, 2 or 3) completes this map of the U.S.A.?

2. **This solid has been made by folding one of the three shapes below (a, b, c). Which one?**

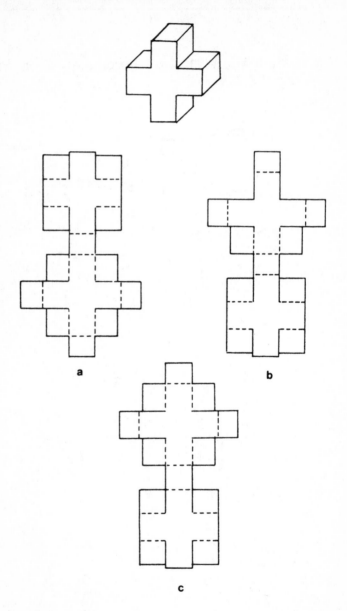

a

b

c

3. How many different arrows are there?

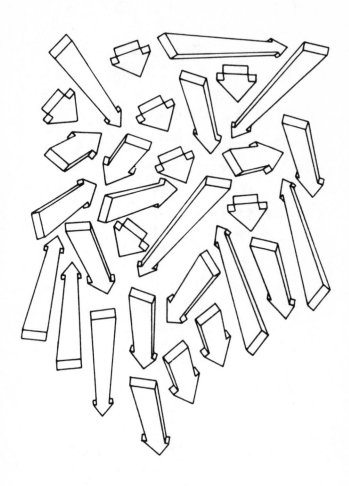

4. **There are two of each of the letters below except one. Which is it?**

5. Spot the difference between these two pictures.

6. Which figure (1, 2, 3) does this shape become when rotated 90° clockwise?

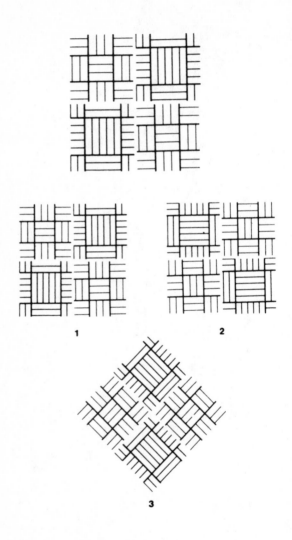

7. How many sides has this solid?

8. How many motorbikes are present, and from how many angles?

9. Spot the difference between these two pictures.

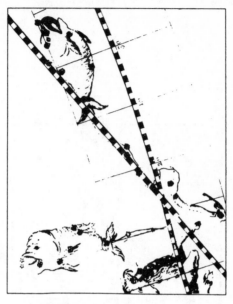

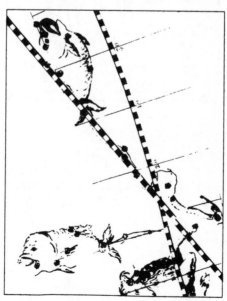

10. Study this chessboard carefully for 30 seconds. Make a mental note of the position of each playing piece. Then cover it up ...

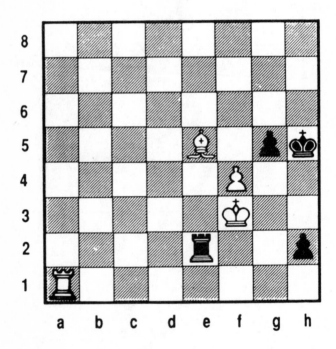

and find the position of the black King from memory.

Logic: problems

1. Which figure completes the sequence?

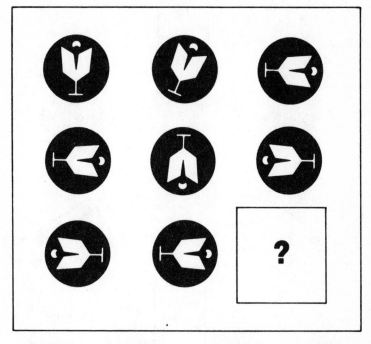

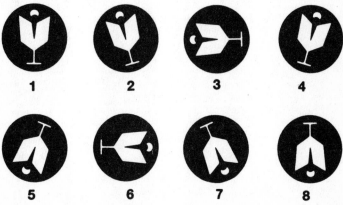

2. Fill in the missing domino.

3. **Which figure, of the six shown, completes the sequence?**

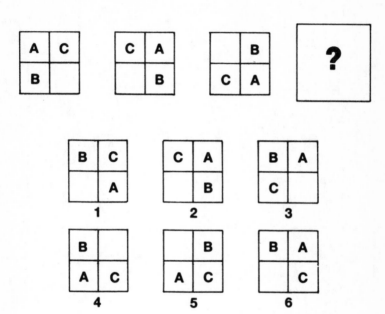

4. Which figure completes the sequence?

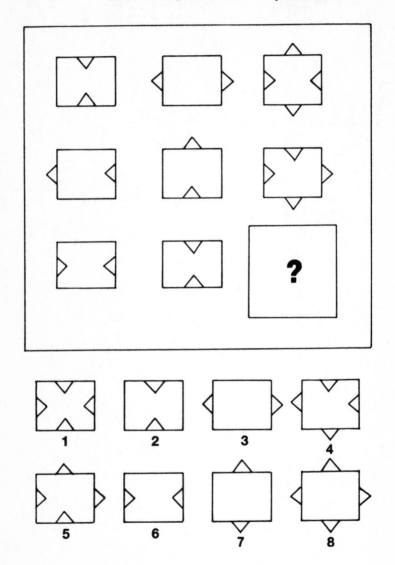

5. What is the hidden card?

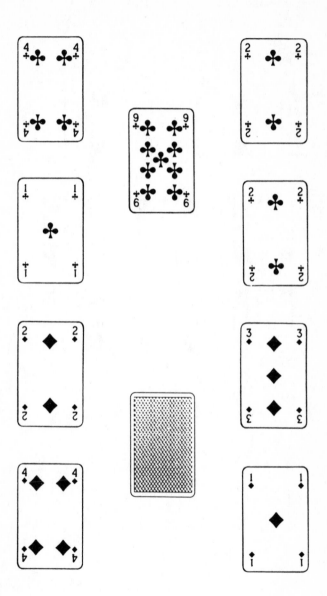

6. Which figure, of the six shown, completes the sequence?

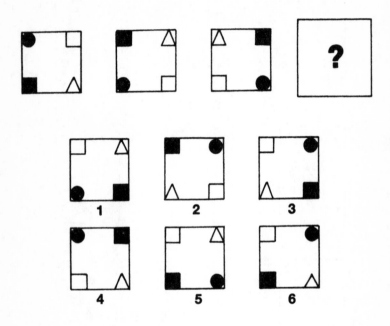

7. Fill in the missing domino.

8. Which figure completes the sequence?

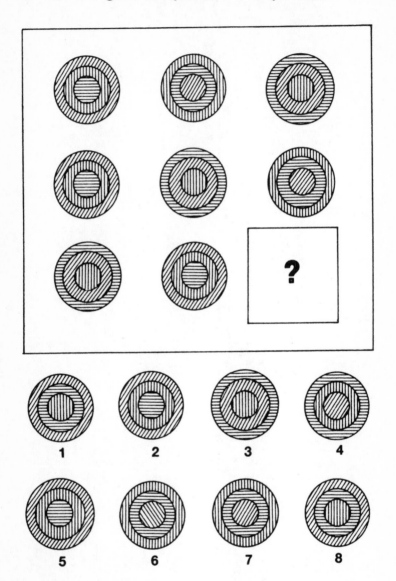

9. Which figure is the odd one out?

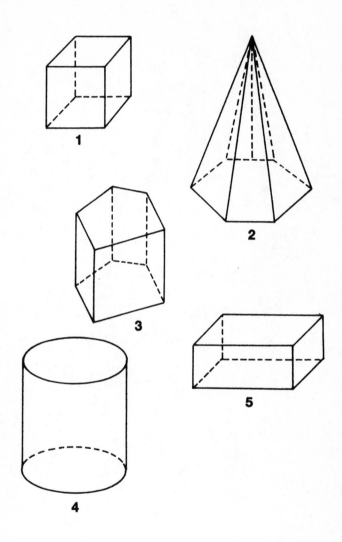

10. What are the missing cards?

Solutions

Numbers

PROBLEM No.	SOLUTION	EXPLANATION
1		In the top triangle, the numbers progress by following the pattern ×2 and then +3 alternately: 2 (×2=) 4 (+3=) 7 (×2=) 14 (+3=) 17. In the bottom triangle, the numbers follow the progression ×3, and then +2 alternately: 3 (×3=) 9 (+2=) 11 (×3=) 33 (+2=) 35.
2	60 and 68	On each line, the second number is equal to the cube of the first number, minus itself. The third number is equal to the cube of the first number, plus itself: $(2^3) = 8 - 2 = (6)$ $2^3 = 8 + 2 = (10)$ $(3^3) = 27 - 3 = (24)$ $3^3 = 27 + 3 = (30)$ $(4^3) = 64 - 4 = (60)$ $4^3 = 64 + 4 = (68)$.
3	8	In each circle, the bottom number is obtained by subtracting the right hand number from the left hand number: $5 - 3 = 2$, $9 - 4 = 5$ and $11 - 3 = 8$.

PROBLEM No.	SOLUTION	EXPLANATION
4	┌─────┐ │ 10 │ ├─────┤ │ 100 │ └─────┘	Starting with the 2 at the top left and alternating top and bottom, the numbers increase by 2 each time. Following the same pattern, the numbers in the other halves are the numbers in the first halves, squared.
5	3	On each line, the right hand number is obtained by adding together the first two numbers and dividing the result by the third number: $8 \times 3 = 24/4 = 6$ $5 \times 4 = 20/10 = 2$ $9 \times 2 = 18/6 = 3$
6	11	The numbers progress following the pattern $+3$, alternating with -1: $4 (+3=) 7 (-1=) 6 (+3=) 9 (-1=) 8 (+3=) 11$.
7	200	The number in brackets is obtained by adding together the two numbers either side and multiplying the result by 2: $21 + 37 = 58 \times 2 = 116$ $27 + 73 = 100 \times 2 = 200$.
8	28	The base number is obtained by multiplying together the two side numbers, and dividing the result by the centre number: $12 \times 6 = 72/4 = 18$ $8 \times 10 = 80/5 = 16$ $4 \times 14 = 56/2 = 28$
9	16	On each line, the right hand number is obtained

PROBLEM No.	SOLUTION	EXPLANATION
		by subtracting the second number from the first, and multiplying the result by the second number again: $7 - 4 = 3 \Rightarrow 4 \times 3 = 12$ $9 - 7 = 2 \Rightarrow 7 \times 2 = 14$ $8 - 4 = 4 \Rightarrow 4 \times 4 = 16$
10	52	In the second circle the numbers are obtained by dividing the numbers in the first circle by 2. In the third circle, the numbers are obtained by multiplying the numbers in the first circle by 2: $8 \times 2 = 16$, $14 \times 2 = 28$, $26 \times 2 = 52$.

Language

PROBLEM No.	SOLUTION	EXPLANATION
1	vice	Which forms the words: novice, service, advice and device.
2	moreover	Rome is an anagram of the first four letters and rove an anagram of the second four.
3	error	The first and third letters of the word in brackets are the last and fifth letters of the right hand word. The second, fourth and fifth letters are the first, fourth and fifth letters of the left hand word.
4	tan	Which forms the words: titan and tango.
5	crossbow	An arrow is a projectile used by a crossbow, just as a bullet is in a rifle.

PROBLEM No.	SOLUTION	EXPLANATION
6	enrich	The others are synonyms.
7	son	Which forms the words: parson and sonnet.
8	GRITE	When the anagrams are solved, tiger is the only mammal, the others being fish: sole, salmon, tuna.
9	wake	A synonym of sequel and funeral.
10	allow	Which forms the words: callow, fallow, hallow, mallow, sallow and wallow.

Perception

PROBLEM No.	SOLUTION
1	Figure 2 completes this map of the U.S.A.
2	Unfolded, the shape becomes figure 'b'.
3	There are six different sizes of arrow.
4	The only Hebrew letter that does not have a double is the second from the top on the left.
5	The '10' is missing on the right thigh of the woman in the second picture.
6	When rotated 90° to the right, the shape becomes figure two.
7	The solid has 30 sides.
8	There are 20 bikes from four angles.
9	A star is missing in the mouth of the fish at the bottom left of the second picture.

PROBLEM No.	SOLUTION
10	The position is remembered by memorising the coordinates h5.

Logic

PROBLEM No.	SOLUTION	EXPLANATION
1		3 Starting on the first line, the figures turn 45° to the right each time. On the second line, they turn 90°, and on the third line 180°.
2	5/4 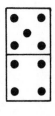	Starting with the top 1, and alternating interior, exterior in a clockwise direction, the numbers increase with one number omitted each time. The same is true with the other halves, but this time the numbers decrease with one number omitted each time. 1 (2) 3 (4) 5 (6) 0 (1) 2 (3) 4 and: 1 (0) 6 (5) 4 (3) 2 (1) 0 (6) 5
3		4 'A' moves one place clockwise each time. B and C move anticlockwise.

PROBLEM No.	SOLUTION	EXPLANATION

4   **8**

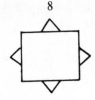

On each line, the right hand figure is obtained by superimposing the two preceding ones. Interior triangles become exterior, and vice-versa.

5   Ten of Diamonds

Two groups of five cards are present; Clubs and Diamonds. The number on the centre card of each group is equal to the sum of the other four cards added together:

$4 + 2 + 1 + 2 = 9$
$2 + 3 + 4 + 1 = 10$

6   **3**

The black circle and the triangle move anti-clockwise. The white and black squares move clockwise.

7   **6/5**

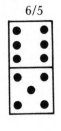

The picture is made up of two groups of three dominoes, either side of the double 0. In each group, the two exterior numbers at the top and bottom are the same. On each domino, the difference between the dominoes' values is always equal to 1:

1/0, 4/3, 2/1
5/4, 3/2, ?/(5)
and:
$1 - 0 = 4 - 3 = 2 - 1 = 1$
$5 - 4 = 3 - 2 = (6) - 5 = 1$

PROBLEM No.	SOLUTION	EXPLANATION

8 7 On each line, the same three patterns are present (vertical, horizontal and diagonal stripes) in a different order each time.

9  4 The cylinder is the only shape without a right angle.

10 Six of Diamonds

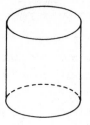

Nine of Diamonds

All the cards are Diamonds. Starting with the Ace and moving clockwise while alternating interior/exterior, the sequence is that of odd numbers. Starting with the two and following the same pattern, the other cards increase by two each time.

Your performance

Award yourself one point for each correct answer and write your different scores into the table below.

WEEKEND FOUR	
PERCEPTION	Number of questions: 10 Correct answers:
LANGUAGE	Number of questions: 10 Correct answers:
LOGIC	Number of questions: 10 Correct answers:
NUMBERS	Number of questions: 10 Correct answers:
	TOTAL QUESTIONS: 40 TOTAL ANSWERS: . .

Refer to the I.Q. curve on page 104 in the chapter 'Assess Yourself'. Work out your intellect level and the progress you are making.

YOUR LEVEL OF
ATTAINMENT

The time has come to work out your score and assess yourself. Having completed all the exercises, you can now take advantage of three different assessements:
— The first one concerns the long programme.
— The second one concerns your intellectual curve.
— The third, your performance curve.
These three assessments are necessary if you are to judge your progress and any possible difficulties you might have.

Long programme: your results

Write your different scores into the table below. Don't forget to mark in the number of wrong answers you made, weekend by weekend, subject by subject, for these are essential in working out your performance curve.

The last line on this table, entitled 'I.Q.' will give you a good idea of how your intellectual level has progressed during the long programme.

	Weekend 1	Weekend 2	Weekend 3	Weekend 4
PERCEPTION	No. of questions: 10 Correct answers: ...	No. of questions: 10 Correct answers: ...	No. of questions: 10 Correct answers: ...	No. of questions: 10 Correct answers: ...
LANGUAGE	No. of questions: 10 Correct answers: ...	No. of questions: 10 Correct answers: ...	No. of questions: 10 Correct answers: ...	No. of questions: 10 Correct answers: ...
LOGIC	No. of questions: 10 Correct answers: ...	No. of questions: 10 Correct answers: ...	No. of questions: 10 Correct answers: ...	No. of questions: 10 Correct answers: ...
NUMBERS	No. of questions: 10 Correct answers: ...	No. of questions: 10 Correct answers: ...	No. of questions: 10 Correct answers: ...	No. of questions: 10 Correct answers: ...
	Total questions: 40 Total answers: ... I.Q. ...	Total questions: 40 Total answers: ... I.Q. ...	Total questions: 40 Total answers: ... I.Q. ...	Total questions: 40 Total answers: ... I.Q. ...

Your intellectual curve

Write your different I.Q. scores into the table below. Join the dots to give you your intellectual curve. (see example).

I.Q.

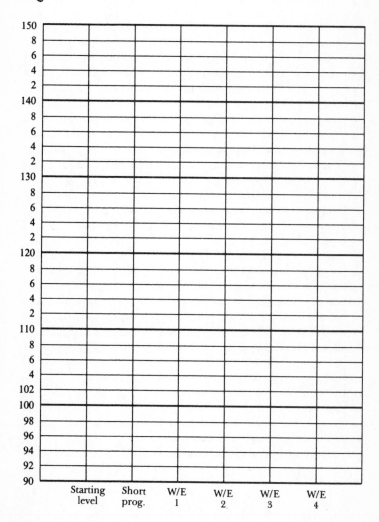

Example:
This example corresponds to an initial I.Q. of 102 (1st I.Q. test), then 108 (short programme), then 106 (1st weekend), 112 (2nd weekend), 119 (3rd weekend) and 134 (4th weekend).

I.Q.

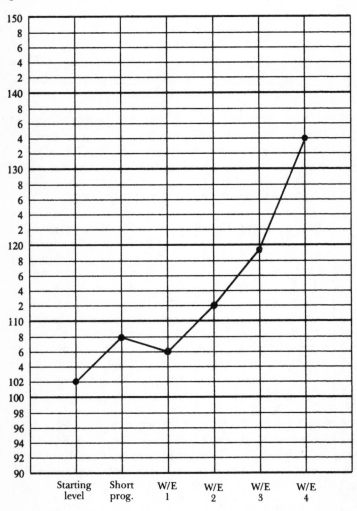

Your performance curve

You can work out a performance curve for each subject. This is the best method of judging the progress you have made, and seeing what remains for you to accomplish.

To establish these curves, the first thing to do is to mark down all your scores on the same scale. To do that you must convert the results you obtained in the first tests ('Assess Yourself' and 'Short Programme') into standard points (base 10). The subsequent scores (Long Programme) are already expressed in this way. Refer yourself to the conversion tables. Subject by subject, they give you the connection between results (see tables at the end of chapters 'Assess Yourself' and 'Short Programme') and standard points.

Once you have done these conversions, you can establish your performance curves by using the table below as an example.

Standard points

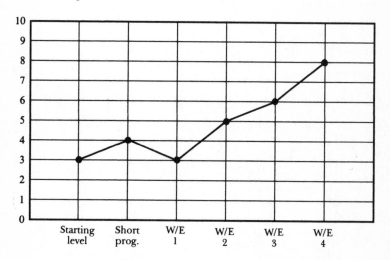

This curve is based on the following scores in the subject 'Numbers': three standard points (four correct answers) in the first test ('Assess Yourself') then four standard points (six correct answers) in the Short Programme, then three standard points* (three correct answers) in the first weekend, then five standard points (five correct answers) in the second weekend, then six standard points in the third weekend and eight standard points in the fourth weekend.

CONVERSION TABLES

I. Assess Yourself

Your results (Number of correct answers)	Standard Points			
	LOGIC (24 problems)	PERCEPTION (16 problems)	LANGUAGE (26 problems)	NUMBERS (14 problems)
1	0	0	0	0
2	1	1	0	1
3	1	2	1	2
4	2	3	1	3
5	2	3	2	4
6	2	4	2	4
7	3	4	3	5
8	3	5	3	6
9	4	5	3	6
10	4	6	4	7
11	5	7	4	8
12	5	7	5	9
13	5	8	5	9
14	6	9	5	10
15	6	9	6	
16	7	10	6	
17	7		7	
18	7		7	
19	8		7	
20	8		8	
21	9		8	
22	9		8	
23	10		9	
24	10		9	
25			10	
26			10	

II. Short Programme

Your results (Number of correct answers)	Standard Points			
	LOGIC (15 problems)	PERCEPTION (15 problems)	LANGUAGE (15 problems)	NUMBERS (15 problems)
1	0	0	0	0
2	1	1	1	1
3	2	2	2	2
4	3	3	3	3
5	3	3	3	3
6	4	4	4	4
7	5	5	5	5
8	5	5	5	5
9	6	6	6	6
10	7	7	7	7
11	7	7	7	7
12	8	8	8	8
13	8	8	8	8
14	9	9	9	9
15	10	10	10	10

* A drop in your score for any given subject is normal during the Long Programme if this subject is the last in the series. With each test having a time limit, the number of 'no answers' can increase in the last series of exercises.

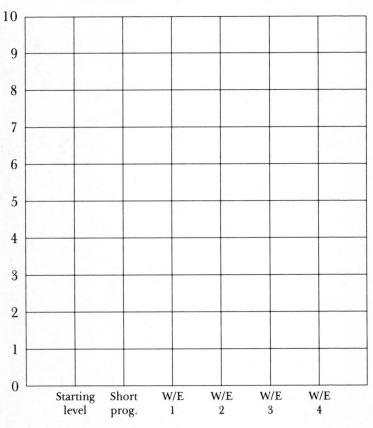

Performance Curve: PERCEPTION

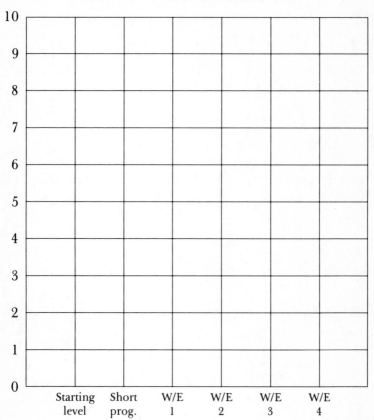

Performance Curve: LANGUAGE

Performance Curve: LOGIC

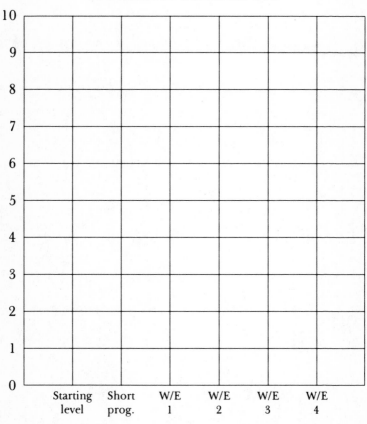

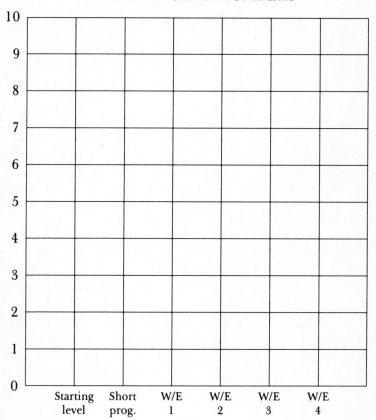

Performance Curve: **NUMBERS**

How to improve your performance

There are several ways to improve your performance:

— By training regularly. See, for example, the series of problems posed in the companion volumes in this series, *Measure Your I.Q.* and *Succeed at I.Q. Tests.*

— By assiduously doing the games, crosswords, puzzles and anagrams found in newspapers and magazines.

— By changing your relationship with the environment. You must understand that all your senses: sight, hearing, smell, touch and taste, take in and store in the memory, thousands of pieces of information. We know, for example, that by stimulating certain parts of the brain we can make someone re-live long gone scenes and events hitherto forgotten, to the extent that they can describe the smallest details as if they were watching a film. Make it a habit, therefore, consciously to watch, listen, touch, smell and taste everything around you.

Try, for example, to build up a picture from memory of your environment, your home, your office, your street and district. Picture them, putting everything in its correct position, room by room, street by street, including every detail of the whole area.

Get accustomed to recapitulating from memory everything you have done that day; all the places you visited, the people you met and the exchanges you had. This may be difficult to begin with, but after a few weeks you will be amazed to find your judgements gaining precision, speed and clarity.

— By changing and revitalising your activities and ideas. Force yourself to see and understand things from someone else's point of view. A good way to do this is to become your own contradictor, to do the opposite of what you would normally do, say or think. Routine is a form of sclerosis, as is lack of cerebral activity. Don't let your brain work on empty, turning over the same old problems and ideas.

Provide it with material: lectures, shows, reports, information and reflections. In general, all these entertainments and new situations are excellent for stimulating cerebral activity.

— By disposing of as many accessories as possible (calculators, memos, etc.). Learn to retain things from memory; train yourself to calculate things in your head by visualising the elements, words and numbers you have to work with. This is the best method of memorising and performing mathematical exercises, planning a presentation and so forth.

— By developing your verbal comprehension and increasing your vocabulary. Most of the time we only have a vague comprehension of the words we use every day. Look up in a dictionary, the meaning of the words you use, even if it appears obvious. You will find there is often a much deeper, sometimes different meaning from what you thought at first. A good dictionary is an excellent bedside book and contains a wealth of information.

— By always working to the limits of your abilities. To conquer without danger is to triumph without glory or profit. You will learn more from losing a game of chess or tennis against someone much better than you, or giving in to a particularly difficult exercise, than by cruising through something easy.

— By leading a healthy lifestyle. This essentially means eating a balanced diet and sleeping well. All food deficiencies (vitamins, minerals, proteins, etc.) and lack of sleep have a negative effect on the brain's chemistry, and considerably reduce intellectual performance. It is in your own interests, therefore, to know your body and its needs precisely, and to take the correct measures to look after it.

— By avoiding excess use of stimulants. Coffee, alcohol and tobacco all have a slight stimulative effect on the brain, but taken in large quantities or over a long period of time, they are depressants.

Vitamin C is a much more powerful and beneficial stimulant if you need a boost during a short period of time brought about by exams, work pressure, or the many other temporary stresses of modern life.).